BASIC

# English Grammar

### FOURTH EDITION

## WORKBOOK

### VOLUME A

*Betty S. Azar*

*Stacy A. Hagen*

**Basic English Grammar, Fourth Edition**
**Workbook Volume A**

Azar Associates: Shelley Hartle, Editor, and Sue Van Etten, Manager

Pearson Education, 10 Bank Street, White Plains, NY 10606

Staff credits: The people who made up the ***Basic English Grammar,
Fourth Edition, Workbook Volume A*** team, representing editorial,
production, design, and manufacturing, are Dave Dickey,
Nancy Flaggman, Amy McCormick, Robert Ruvo, and
Marian Wassner.

Text composition: S4Carlisle Publishing Services

Illustrations: Don Martinetti and Chris Pavely

Printed in the United States of America

ISBN 10:    0-13-294226-7
ISBN 13: 978-0-13-294226-3

3  17

For Julianna

-S. H.

# Contents

The titles listed below, for example, *Singular pronouns* + *be*, refer to section names, not practice titles. In general, one section has multiple exercises.
The chart numbers refer to the grammar explanations in the *Basic English Grammar*
**Student Book**.

# Preface

The *Basic English Grammar Workbook* is a self-study textbook. It is keyed to the explanatory grammar charts found in *Basic English Grammar, Fourth Edition,* a classroom teaching text for English language learners. Students can use the *Workbook* independently to enhance their understanding of English structures. Practice ranges from the basic to the more challenging so students can choose from a variety of exercises that will help them use English meaningfully and correctly.

This *Workbook* is also a resource for teachers who need exercise material for additional classwork, homework, testing, or individualized instruction.

The answers to the practices can be found in the *Answer Key* in the back of the *Workbook.* Its pages are perforated so that they can be detached to make a separate booklet. However, if teachers want to use the *Workbook* as a classroom teaching text, the *Answer Key* can be removed at the beginning of the term.

# Chapter 1
## Using Be

▶ **Practice 1. Using *he, she,* or *it.*** (Chart 1-1)
Rewrite each sentence using the correct pronoun: *he*, *she*, or *it*.

1. The bus is here.  _It is here._
2. Sara is late.  _____
3. English is difficult.  _____
4. Mr. Jefferson is sick.  _____
5. Mrs. Jefferson is also sick.  _____
6. Henry is ready.  _____
7. The weather is cold.  _____
8. Ms. Hogan is single.  _____

▶ **Practice 2. Using *am, is,* or *are.*** (Chart 1 1)
Complete each sentence with *am*, *is*, or *are*.

1. She _____ hungry.
2. I _____ sick.
3. You _____ nice.
4. The weather _____ hot.
5. Mr. Kimura _____ old.
6. Julianna _____ young.
7. It _____ cold.
8. You _____ early.
9. Ms. Rossi _____ here.
10. She _____ nervous.

dentist

He is nervous.

▶ **Practice 3. Singular and plural pronouns.** (Charts 1-1 and 1-2)
Choose the correct picture.

       **A**            **B**

1. I am here. _____*A*_____

2. You are sick. _____*A, B*_____

3. They are ready. _____

4. We are tired. _____

5. She is from Canada. _____

6. You are late. _____

▶ **Practice 4. Pronoun + *be*.** (Charts 1-1 and 1-2)
Create your own chart by completing the sentences with a form of *be*.

1. I _____*am*_____ cold.     6. You (two) _____ cold.

2. You (one) _____ cold.     7. We _____ cold.

3. He _____ cold.     8. You and I _____ cold.

4. She _____ cold.     9. They _____ cold.

5. It _____ cold.     10. You and they _____ cold.

▶ **Practice 5. Pronoun + *be*.** (Charts 1-1 and 1-2)
Complete the sentences with the correct pronouns.

1. Jack and Bruno are homesick. _____*They*_____ are homesick.

2. Bruno is homesick. _____*He*_____ is homesick.

3. Julia is homesick. _____ is homesick.

4. Mr. Rivas is homesick. _____ is homesick.

5. Mrs. Rivas is homesick. _____ is homesick.

6. Mrs. Rivas and Mr. Rivas are homesick. _____ are homesick.

7. Mr. Rivas and I are homesick. _____ are homesick.

8. You and I are homesick. _____ are homesick.

9. Jenna is happy. _____ is happy.

10. You and Jenna are happy. _____ are happy.

11. The children are happy. _____ are happy.

12. Dr. Chen is ready. Dr. Greco is ready. _____ are ready.

13. Ella is ready. _____ is ready.

14. Brian is ready. _____ is ready.

15. Ella, Brian, and I are ready. _____ are ready.

▶ **Practice 6. *A* or *an*.** (Chart 1-3)
Write *a* or *an* before each word.

1. ___*an*___ office

2. _____ boy

3. _____ desk

4. _____ apple

5. _____ city

6. _____ animal

7. _____ ear

8. _____ letter

9. _____ table

10. _____ insect

INSECTS

a bee

a fly

an ant

a mosquito

▶ **Practice 7. *A* or *an*.** (Chart 1-3)
Complete the sentences with *a* or *an*. Then choose *yes* or *no*.

1. Chinese is ___*a*___ language.          (yes)     no

2. Paris is _____ city.          yes     no

3. Canada is _____ continent.          yes     no

4. Hawaii is _____ island.          yes     no

5. Africa is _____ place.          yes     no

6. English is _____ country.          yes     no

7. French is _____ language.          yes     no

8. Asia is _____ continent.          yes     no

► **Practice 8. Plural nouns.** (Chart 1-4)
Write the plural forms for the given nouns.

| Singular | | Plural |
|---|---|---|
| 1. a city | → | _cities_ |
| 2. a dog | → | _____ |
| 3. a language | → | _____ |
| 4. a machine | → | _____ |
| 5. a country | → | _____ |
| 6. a season | → | _____ |
| 7. a dictionary | → | _____ |

► **Practice 9. A, an, or Ø.** (Charts 1-3 and 1-4)
Write complete sentences using **is/are** and **a/an/Ø** (nothing).

1. A bee \ insect      _A bee is an insect._

2. Ant \ insect      _Ants are insects._

3. Russian and Spanish \ language _____

4. China \ country _____

5. South America \ continent _____

6. Dogs \ animal _____

7. Bangkok \ city _____

8. Thailand \ country _____

► **Practice 10. Singular and plural nouns.** (Charts 1-3 and 1-4)
Complete the words with **-s** or Ø.

1. A lion _Ø_ is an animal _Ø_ .

         a lion

2. Lion _s_ are animals _s_ .

3. Korean ____ is a language ____ .

4. An air conditioner ____ is a machine ____ .

5. Tulip ____ are flower ____ .

         a tulip

6. A fly ____ is an insect ____ .

7. Flies ____ are insect ____ .

8. Spring ____ and summer ____ are season ____ .

9. Soccer _____ and tennis _____ are sport _____.

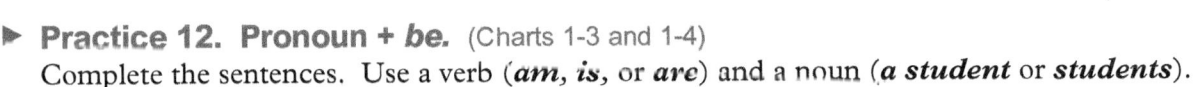

▶ **Practice 11. *Be* with singular and plural nouns.** (Charts 1-3 and 1-4)
Choose the correct verb.

1. Mosquitos   (*is* /(*are*))   insects.

2. A chicken   (*is* / *are*)   an animal.

3. Chinese and Russian   (*is* / *are*)   languages.

4. December and January   (*is* / *are*)   months.

5. A refrigerator   (*is* / *are*)   a machine.

6. Refrigerators   (*is* / *are*)   machines.

7. Bali   (*is* / *are*)   an island.

8. Indonesia and Malaysia   (*is* / *are*)   countries.

9. Carrots   (*is* / *are*)   vegetables.

10. Winter   (*is* / *are*)   a season.

11. Horses   (*is* / *are*)   animals.

a refrigerator

a horse

▶ **Practice 12. Pronoun + *be*.** (Charts 1-3 and 1-4)
Complete the sentences. Use a verb (***am, is,*** or ***are***) and a noun (***a student*** or ***students***).

1. She ___*is a student*_____.

2. I _____.

3. You (one person) _____.

4. You (two persons) _____.

5. They _____.

6. He _____.

7. We _____.

8. Carlos and you _____.

9. He and I _____.

10. Mia and I _____.

▶ **Practice 13. _Be_ with singular and plural nouns.** (Charts 1-3 and 1-4)
Write complete sentences. Use a verb (_is_ or _are_). Use the singular or plural form of the noun.

1. Asia \ continent      _Asia is a continent._

2. Africa \ continent      _____

3. Asia and Africa \ continent      _____

4. Paris \ city      _____

5. Cairo \ city      _____

6. Paris and Cairo \ city      _____

7. Malaysia \ country      _____

8. Japan and Malaysia \ country      _____

▶ **Practice 14. _Be_ with singular and plural.** (Charts 1-3 and 1-4)
Complete the sentences with _is_ or _are_ and one of the nouns from the box. Use the correct singular form of the noun (with _a_ or _an_) or the correct plural form.

| animal | country | language |
|---|---|---|
| city | insect | machine |

1. A dog _____ _is an animal_ _____.

2. Dogs _____ _are animals_ _____.

3. Spanish _____.

4. Spanish and Chinese _____.

5. Thailand and Vietnam _____.

6. Thailand _____.

7. A butterfly _____.

8. Butterflies _____.

9. A car _____.

10. Cars _____.

11. Berlin _____.

12. Berlin and Baghdad _____.

a butterfly

► **Practice 15. Contractions with *be*.** (Chart 1-5)
Write the contraction.

1. I am _____I'm_____        5. it is _____

2. you are _____     6. they are _____

3. he is _____       7. she is _____

4. we are _____

► **Practice 16. Negative forms of *be*.** (Chart 1-6)
Complete the sentences with the negative form of *be*.

1. I ___am not___ sick.            7. We _____ sick.

2. You _____ sick.       8. They _____ sick.

3. He _____ sick.        9. The students _____ sick.

4. She _____ sick.       10. Katie and I _____ sick.

5. The cat _____ sick.   11. The teacher _____ sick.

6. It _____ sick.        12. The teachers _____ sick.

► **Practice 17. Negative forms of *be* and contractions.** (Chart 1-6)
Complete the sentences with the negative form of *be*. Then write the contracted form. Give
both forms where possible.

| | ***Be:* Negative** | | **Contraction** |
|---|---|---|---|
| 1. You | _____are not_____ | late. | _____aren't_ OR _you're not_____ |
| 2. She | _____ | late. | _____ |
| 3. I | _____ | late. | _____ |
| 4. He | _____ | late. | _____ |
| 5. The bus | _____ | late. | _____ |
| 6. It | _____ | late. | _____ |
| 7. We | _____ | late. | _____ |
| 8. You | _____ | late. | _____ |
| 9. They | _____ | late. | _____ |

► **Practice 18. Using *is, isn't, are,* or *aren't*.** (Charts 1-5 and 1-6)
Complete the sentences with *is, isn't, are,* or *aren't*.

1. Canada and Sweden _____*aren't*_____ continents.

2. Japan _____ a language.

3. A computer _____ a machine.

4. Tennis _____ a season.

5. Bees _____ insects.

6. Carrots _____ animals.

7. A rabbit _____ an animal.

8. Seoul and Beijing _____ cities.

9. Refrigerators _____ continents.

10. Greenland _____ a city.

a rabbit

► **Practice 19. Using *be*.** (Charts 1-5 and 1-6)
Complete the sentences with the correct information. Use a form of *be* with a contraction.

1. Korea _____*isn't*_____ a city. It *'s a country*_____.

2. Computers _____ insects. They _____.

3. Asia _____ a continent. It _____ a country.

4. Spring and summer _____ sports. They _____.

5. Arabic _____ a country. It _____.

6. I _____ an English teacher. I _____.

7. We _____ students. We _____ English students.

► **Practice 20. *Be* + adjective.** (Chart 1-7)
Complete the sentences with the correct information. Use *is, isn't, are,* or *aren't*.

1. A mouse _____*isn't*_____ big.

2. A diamond _____ cheap.

3. Diamonds _____ expensive.

4. Bananas _____ expensive.

5. The earth _____ flat. It _____ round.

6. English grammar _____ hard. It _____ easy.

7. This exercise _____ difficult. It _____ easy.

8. Flowers _____ ugly. They _____ beautiful.

9. Traffic at rush hour _____ noisy. It _____ quiet.

10. Ice cream and candy _____ sour. They _____ sweet.

▶ **Practice 21. *Be* + adjective.** (Charts 1-5 → 1-7)
Write complete sentences using *is/isn't* or *are/aren't* and the given words.

1. apples . . . blue / red

    _____*Apples aren't blue.  They're red.*_____

2. a circle . . . round / square

    _____

3. a piano . . . heavy / light

    _____

4. potato chips . . . sweet / salty

    _____

5. the Sahara Desert . . . large / small

    _____

6. the Nile River . . . short / long

    _____

7. this exercise . . . easy / difficult

    _____

8. my grammar book . . . new / old

    _____

9. electric cars . . . expensive / cheap

    _____

a piano

► **Practice 22. Identifying prepositions.** (Chart 1-8)
Write the preposition in the blank. Underline the prepositional phrase in each sentence.

**Preposition**

1. _____*in*_____     David is <u>in his office</u>.

2. _____     Mr. Han is at the train station.

3. _____     Karim is from Kuwait.

4. _____     My book is on my desk.

5. _____     Lily's wallet is in her purse.

6. _____     The post office is on First Street.

7. _____     The post office is next to the bank.

8. _____     My feet are under my desk.

9. _____     My nose is between my cheeks.

10. _____     My apartment is on the third floor.

11. _____     It is above Mr. Kwan's apartment.


► **Practice 23. Understanding prepositions.** (Chart 1-8)
Follow the instructions.

Put an "X" . . .

1. above circle A.

2. under circle B.

3. in circle A.

4. between circles A and B.

5. next to circle A.


► **Practice 24. Review: nouns, adjectives, and prepositions.** (Chart 1-9)
Write the words in the correct columns on the next page.

| | | | |
|---|---|---|---|
| ✓ at | ✓ easy | next to | single |
| between | empty | on | sister |
| ✓ city | happy | outside | teacher |
| country | hungry | parents | |

| Nouns | Adjectives | Prepositions (of Place) |
|-------|-----------|------------------------|
| _city_ | _easy_ | _at_ |
| | | |
| | | |
| | | |
| | | |

▶ **Practice 25. Sentence review.** (Chart 1-9)
Complete the sentences using the given structure.

1. Dr. John Brown is (*noun*) _____ _a dentist / a doctor, etc._ _____.

   (*place*) _____ _here / at home, etc._ _____.

   (*adjective*) _____ _friendly / nice, etc._ _____.

2. Anna is (*noun*) _____.

   (*place*) _____.

   (*adjective*) _____.

3. Russia is (*adjective*) _____.

   (*place*) _____.

   (*noun*) _____.

4. *Basic English Grammar Workbook* is (*place*) _____.

   (*adjective*) _____.

   (*noun*) _____.

▶ **Practice 26. Sentence review.** (Chart 1-9)
Make true sentences using the given words and a form of **be**.

1. Canada \ a city

   _Canada isn't a city._

2. Canada \ in North America

   _____

3. France \ next to \ Germany

   _____

4. The downstairs of a building \ above \ the upstairs

_____

5. Ice \ hot

_____

6. apples and oranges \ vegetables

_____

7. airplanes \ fast

_____

8. vegetables \ healthy

_____

9. an alligator \ dangerous

_____

10. alligators \ friendly

_____

an alligator

▶ **Practice 27. Review of *be*.** (Chapter 1)
Complete the sentences with the correct form of *be*.

Kara and Tia ___*are*___ from Greece. They _____ new students. Mrs. Kemper
           1                                    2
_____ the teacher. She _____ very nice. Fifteen students _____ in the class.
    3                    4                                        5
They _____ friendly. Kara and Tia _____ happy in this class.
     6                                7

▶ **Practice 28. Review of *be*.** (Chapter 1)
Complete the sentences with the correct form of *be*.

MR. QUINN:  Hi, I ___*am*___ Mr. Quinn. Mrs. Kemper _____ not here.
                   1                                  2

            She _____ sick. I _____ your teacher today.
                 3              4

KARA:       Hi, my name _____ Kara.
                         5

MR. QUINN:  Hi, Kara. It _____ nice to meet you.
                         6

KARA:       I _____ happy to meet you too. This _____ my sister, Tia.
               7                                      8

MR. QUINN:  Hi, Tia. I _____ glad* to meet you too.
                        9

_____

*glad* = happy.

# Chapter 2
## Using Be and Have

▶ **Practice 1. Yes/no questions with be.** (Chart 2-1)
Choose the correct completion.

1. ____ you happy?
   a. Am    b. Is    c. Are

2. ____ they here?
   a. Am    b. Is    c. Are

3. ____ he absent?
   a. Am    b. Is    c. Are

4. ____ she a teacher?
   a. Am    b. Is    c. Are

5. ____ I late?
   a. Am    b. Is    c. Are

6. ____ we ready?
   a. Am    b. Is    c. Are

7. ____ you and Paul ready?
   a. Am    b. Is    c. Are

8. ____ Roberto and Elena at home?
   a. Am    b. Is    c. Are

9. ____ Emily here?
   a. Am    b. Is    c. Are

10. ____ you from Canada?
    a. Am    b. Is    c. Are

▶ **Practice 2. Yes/no questions with be.** (Chart 2-1)
Make yes/no questions with the given words and a form of *be*.

1. you \ a student _____Are you a student?_____

2. he \ a student _____

3. they \ students _____

4. she \ from New Zealand _____

5. you \ ready _____

6. we \ ready _____

7. it \ ready _____

8. I \ ready _____

► **Practice 3. Yes/no questions with be.** (Chart 2-1)
Make questions for the given answers.

1. A: _____*Are you a doctor?*_____
   B: Yes, I am a doctor.

2. A: _____
   B: Yes, bananas are healthy.

3. A: _____
   B: Yes, Taka is a nurse.

4. A: _____
   B: Yes, the kids are at school.

5. A: _____
   B: Yes, we are ready for the test.

6. A: _____
   B: Yes, Liz is at school.

7. A: _____
   B: Yes, I am tired.

► **Practice 4. Short answers with be.** (Chart 2-2)
Complete the sentences with short answers.

1. Is Paris a city?              Yes, _____*it is*_____.

2. Are Paris and Tokyo cities?   Yes, _____.

3. Are dogs animals?             Yes, _____.

4. Is Carlos sick today?         Yes, _____.

5. Are apples fruits?            Yes, _____.

6. Is the sun hot?               Yes, _____.

7. Is Jane a teacher?            Yes, _____.

8. Are you a student?            Yes, _____.

9. Are you students?             Yes, _____.

10. Am I early?                  Yes, _____.

► **Practice 5. Questions and short answers with be.** (Chart 2-2)
Complete the questions and answers.

Anna
an English teacher

Mr. Sanchez
an English student

Susan
a photographer

Mrs. Brown
a police officer

Joe
a college student

1. ____*Is*____ Mr. Sanchez a student? Yes, he ____*is*____.

2. _____ Anna a teacher? Yes, she _____.

3. _____ Joe a student? Yes, he _____.

4. _____ Susan a photographer? Yes, she _____.

5. _____ Joe and Mr. Sanchez students? Yes, they _____.

6. _____ Mrs. Brown a police officer? Yes, she _____.

7. _____ Anna and Susan women? Yes, they _____.

8. _____ Mr. Sanchez and Joe men? Yes, they _____.

9. _____ you a student? Yes, I _____.

10. _____ you and Mr. Sanchez students? Yes, we _____.

► **Practice 6. Capitalization and punctuation.** (Charts 2-2)
Rewrite the sentences. Add capitals letters and the correct punctuation.

1. is Paris a country    no it isn't

_____

2. are October and November months    yes they are

_____

3. is soccer a season    no it isn't

_____

4. are fall and winter seasons    yes they are

_____


▶ **Practice 7. Questions and short answers with *be*.** (Chart 2-2)
Make questions and give short answers. Use contractions where possible.

```
┌─────────────────────────────┐  ┌─────────────────────────────┐
│   NEW STUDENT INFORMATION   │  │   NEW STUDENT INFORMATION   │
│ ┌─────┐  Name: Rosa Gonzalez│  │ ┌─────┐  Name: Dong Vuong   │
│ │     │                     │  │ │     │                     │
│ │     │  Country: Spain     │  │ │     │  Country: Vietnam   │
│ │     │                     │  │ │     │                     │
│ │     │  Age: 22            │  │ │     │  Age: 24            │
│ └─────┘                     │  │ └─────┘                     │
│      ___male  _X_ female    │  │      _X_ male  ___female    │
└─────────────────────────────┘  └─────────────────────────────┘
```

1. _____*Is*_____ Rosa a student?    Yes, she ____*is*____.

2. ____*Is Dong*____ a teacher?    No, he ____*isn't*____.

3. _____ students?    Yes, _____.

4. _____ from Mexico?    No, she _____.

5. _____ from Vietnam?    Yes, _____.

6. _____ 22?    Yes, _____.

7. _____ 25?    No, he _____.

8. _____ 23?    No, they _____.


▶ **Practice 8. Questions and short answers with *be*.** (Chart 2-2)
Complete the conversations. Use contractions where possible.

1. A: ____*Is*____ Gloria a student?

   B: Yes, ____*she is*____.

   A: _____ a student?

   B: No, I'm not.

2. A: _____ students?

   B: No, we _____. We _____ teachers.

   A: Is Mr. Ito a teacher?

   B: No, _____. He _____ a student.


**16** CHAPTER 2

► **Practice 9. Understanding *where*.** (Chart 2-3)
Choose the correct question for each response.

| **Question** | **Response** |
|---|---|
| 1. a. Where is Toshi?<br> (b.) Is Toshi at work? | Yes, he is. |
| 2. a. Are the students in the cafeteria?<br> b. Where are the students? | They are in the cafeteria. |
| 3. a. Is my grammar book at home?<br> b. Where is my grammar book? | Yes, it is. |
| 4. a. Where are the dictionaries?<br> b. Are the dictionaries in the classroom? | Yes, they are. |
| 5. a. Where are you?<br> b. Are you at home? | I am at home. |
| 6. a. Is the teacher in her office?<br> b. Where is the teacher? | She is in her office. |

► **Practice 10. Questions with *be* and *where*.** (Chart 2-3)
Make questions.

1. A: _____Where is the teacher?_____
   B: In the classroom. (The teacher is in the classroom.)

2. A: _____
   B: Yes, she is. (The teacher is in the classroom.)

3. A: _____
   B: At home. (Pablo and Dina are at home.)

4. A: _____
   B: Yes, they are. (Pablo and Dina are at home.)

5. A: _____
   B: Yes, it is. (The map is in the car.)

6. A: _____
   B: On First Avenue. (The store is on First Avenue.)

7. A: _____
   B: Yes, we are. (We are outside.)

8. A: _____
   B: Outside. (We are outside.)

► **Practice 11. Using *have* and *has*.** (Chart 2-4)
Complete the sentences with the correct form of *have*.

1. I ____*have*____ a book.

2. You _____ a book.

3. She _____ a book.

4. He _____ a book.

5. Mr. Marks _____ a book.

6. The dog _____ a book.

7. It _____ a book.

8. Mrs. Hong _____ a book.

9. They _____ books.

10. The students _____ books.

11. You _____ books.

► **Practice 12. Using *have* and *has*.** (Chart 2-4)
Complete the sentences with *have* or *has*.

1. You ____*have*____ a ruler on your desk.

2. Eric _____ an eraser on his chair.

3. We _____ grammar books.

4. I _____ a grammar book. It _____ a red cover.

5. Lucy _____ a blue pen. She _____ a blue notebook too.

6. Stella and Dave _____ notebooks. They _____ pencils too.

7. Samir is a student in our class. He _____ a laptop computer.

8. You and I are students. We _____ laptops on our desks.

9. Mike _____ a wallet in his pocket. Mira _____ a wallet in her purse.

10. Nadia isn't in class today because she _____ the flu.

11. Mr. and Mrs. Collins _____ two teenagers.

▶ **Practice 13. *Be* and *have*.** (Chapter 1 and Chart 2-4)
Complete each sentence with the correct form of **be** or **have**.

1. My apartment . . .

   a. _____*has*_____ five rooms.

   b. _____*is*_____ comfortable.

   c. _____ in the city.

   d. _____ twenty years old.

   e. _____ a new kitchen.

   f. _____ expensive.

   g. _____ on the fourth floor.

   h. _____ many windows.

   i. _____ a view of downtown.

2. My neighbor . . .

   a. _____ thirty years old.

   b. _____ brown eyes and brown hair.

   c. _____ tall.

   d. _____ two children.

   e. _____ a small apartment.

   f. _____ friendly.

   g. _____ a student at the university.

   h. _____ very busy.

   i. _____ a busy life.

▶ **Practice 14. *Be* and *have*.** (Chapter 1 and Chart 2-4)
Complete each sentence with the correct form of **be** or **have**.

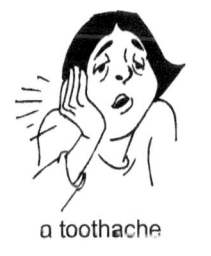

a toothache

1. Jean _____*has*_____ a toothache. She _____*is*_____ at the dentist.

2. Several students _____ absent. They _____ colds.

3. I _____ not at school. I _____ a stomachache.

4. My parents _____ sick. They _____ fevers.

5. Mr. Paul _____ a backache. He _____ at home.

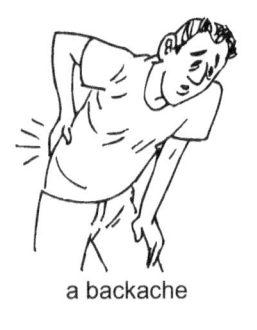

a backache

► **Practice 15. Be and have.** (Chart 2-4)
Complete the sentences with **has**, **have**, **is**, or **are**.

The people in Dr. Lin's waiting room ____are____ sick.  Billy _____ a cold.
<br>                                                       1                                  2

Thomas _____ a stomachache.  Mr. and Mrs. Gleason _____ fevers.
<br>               3                                                   4

Mrs. Martinez _____ a headache.
<br>                    5

The construction workers _____ backaches.
<br>                                6

Nicole _____ a sore throat.
<br>               7

Dr. Lin _____ very busy.
<br>               8

► **Practice 16. Possessive adjectives.** (Chart 2-5)
Complete the sentences.  Use **my**, **your**, **her**, **his**, **our**, or **their**.

a backpack

1.  He has a backpack.  ____His____ backpack is heavy.

2.  You have a backpack.  _____ backpack is heavy.

3.  I have a backpack.  _____ backpack is heavy.

4.  We have backpacks.  _____ backpacks are heavy.

5.  You have backpacks.  _____ backpacks are heavy.

6.  They have backpacks.  _____ backpacks are heavy.

7.  The students have backpacks.  _____ backpacks are heavy.

8.  Tom has a backpack.  _____ backpack is heavy.

9.  Kate has a backpack.  _____ backpack is heavy.

10. Tom and Kate have backpacks.  _____ backpacks are heavy.

11. Kate and I have backpacks.  _____ backpacks are heavy.

12. You and I have backpacks.  _____ backpacks are heavy.

► **Practice 17. Possessive adjectives.** (Chart 2-5)
Use the information in the chart to complete the sentences about the after-school activities of Jenny, Bill, Karen, and Kathy. Use **his**, **her**, or **their**.

Jenny

Bill

Karen

Kathy

Bill

|  | **Jenny** | **Bill** | **Karen and Kathy** |
|---|---|---|---|
| Monday | dance class | soccer practice | baseball game |
| Tuesday |  |  |  |
| Wednesday | piano lesson |  | soccer practice |
| Thursday |  | piano lesson |  |

1. _____*His*_____ soccer practice is on Monday.

2. _____ dance class is on Monday.

3. _____ piano lesson is on Thursday.

4. _____ soccer practice is on Wednesday.

5. _____ piano lesson is on Wednesday.

6. _____ baseball game is on Monday.

► **Practice 18. *Have* and possessive adjectives.** (Chart 2-5)
Complete the sentences. Use **have** or **has** and **my**, **your**, **her**, **his**, **our**, or **their**.

1. I _____*have*_____ a teenage daughter. _____*My*_____ daughter is busy.

2. You _____ homework. _____ homework is easy.

3. Peter and Ellen _____ new cell phones. _____ cell phones are inexpensive.

4. We _____ an old car. _____ car is slow.

5. Hector _____ a mustache. _____ mustache is black.

6. Maria _____ two grandchildren. _____ grandchildren are friendly.

7. Nathan _____ a motorcycle. _____ motorcycle is slow.

a motorcycle

8. Mr. and Mrs. Brown _____ an apartment. _____ apartment is on the top floor.

9. I _____ a dictionary. _____ dictionary is English-Japanese.

10. The workers _____ boots. _____ boots are heavy.

▶ **Practice 19. *This* or *that*.** (Chart 2-6)
Complete the sentences with *this* or *that*.

1. _____*This*_____ is my house key.

2. _____ is your phone card.

3. _____ is your checkbook.

4. _____ is my credit card.

5. _____ is my briefcase.

6. _____ is your bag.

7. _____ is your baseball cap.

8. _____ is my wallet.

► **Practice 20. These or those.** (Chart 2-7)
Complete the sentences with *these* or *those*.

1. ___These___ are apples.

2. _____ are oranges.

3. _____ are pears.

4. _____ are lemons.

5. _____ are bananas.

6. _____ are carrots.

► **Practice 21. This, that, these, and those.** (Charts 2-6 and 2-7)
Choose the correct completion.

1. (*This* / *These*) keys are your house keys.
2. (*That* / *Those*) keys are my car keys.
3. (*This* / *These*) thumb drive is cheap.
4. (*That* / *Those*) thumb drives are expensive.
5. (*That* / *Those*) computer is new.
6. (*This* / *These*) computers are slow.
7. (*This* / *These*) computer is fast.

a thumb drive

► **Practice 22. This, that, these, and those.** (Charts 2-6 and 2-7)
Complete each sentence with *this*, *that*, *these*, or *those*.

1. (*This* / *These*) ___This___ book is inexpensive. (*That* / *Those*) ___Those___
    books are expensive.

2. (*This* / *These*) _____ chairs are comfortable. (*That* / *Those*) _____
    chairs are uncomfortable.

3. (*This* / *These*) _____ car is fast. (*That* / *Those*) _____ car is slow.

4. (*This* / *These*) _____ cats are friendly. (*That* / *Those*) _____ cat is
    unfriendly.

5. (*This / These*) _____ library card is new. (*That / Those*) _____ library card is old.

6. (*This / These*) _____ shoes are comfortable. (*That / Those*) _____ shoes are uncomfortable.

7. (*This / These*) _____ exercise is easy. (*That / Those*) _____ exercises are hard.

▶ **Practice 23. Understanding *who* and *what*.** (Chart 2-8)
Choose the correct response for each question.

1. Who is that?
   (a.) That is Rita.          b. That is a toy.

2. What is that?
   a. That is an electric car.    b. That is Tom.

3. Who are they?
   a. They are flowers.       b. They are new students.

4. What are they?
   a. They are small insects.   b. They are Dick and Mira.

5. Who is this?
   a. This is my new car.     b. This is Kenny.

6. What are they?
   a. They are my children.    b. They are batteries.

batteries

▶ **Practice 24. *Who* and *what* + *be*.** (Chart 2-8)
Make a question with ***who*** or ***what*** for each answer.

1. A: _____*Who is that?*_____
   B: That is the teacher.

2. A: _____
   B: That is medicine.

3. A: _____
   B: These are DVDs.

4. A: _____
   B: They are visitors.

5. A: _____
   B: Those are aspirin.

6. A: _____
   B: That is Dr. Benson.

Aspirin

► **Practice 25. Review: questions and short answers.** (Chapter 2)
Answer the questions. Choose from the responses in the box.

> Yes, it is.        This is Donna.        Yes, I am.
> It's in Norway.     ✓ Yes, they are.       No, it isn't.
> Yes, he is.        This is an insect.      Yes, she is.

1. Are the students smart? _____*Yes, they are.*_____

2. Who is this? _____

3. Is Oslo a city? _____

4. Is Megan a dentist? _____

5. Is Canada a continent? _____

6. Is Charles a teenager? _____

7. Where is Oslo? _____

8. Are you sick? _____

9. What is this? _____

► **Practice 26. *Be* and possessive adjectives.** (Chapters 1 and 2)
Complete the sentences. Use the correct form of *be* and the appropriate possessive adjective.

This is the Jackson family. Pat is the mother. Bob is ___*her*___ husband. They have

two children. _____ children are Karen and Joe. Karen is Joe's sister. Joe is _____

brother. Joe and Bonnie are married. They have one child. Tom is _____ son. _____

grandparents are Pat and Bob.

► **Practice 27. Be and *have*.** (Chapters 1 and 2)
Complete the sentences with the correct forms of **be** and **have**.

I __*have*__ one brother and one sister. My brother _____ a nurse. He _____ a
     1                                   2                     3

good job at a medical clinic. His name _____ Daniel. He _____ 30 years old. My
                                     4                           5

sister _____ a doctor. She _____ very busy. She _____ many patients. Her name
      6                7                    8

_____ Monica. She _____ 35 years old. My name _____ Martha. I _____
  9              10                        11              12

28 years old. I _____ an English teacher. We all _____ good jobs. We _____
             13                             14                15

happy with our work.

► **Practice 28. Be and *have*.** (Chapters 1 and 2)
Complete the sentences with information about your life.

1. My name _____ .

2. I _____ from _____ .

3. _____ a student.

4. My classes are _____ .

5. _____ and _____ are two of my friends.

6. My family is _____ .

7. My father is _____ .

8. My mother is _____ .

9. I _____ (*single/married*).

10. I have _____ (*an apartment/a house/a dorm room/a roommate*).

# Chapter 3

## Using the Simple Present

▶ **Practice 1. Form of the simple present tense.** (Chart 3-1)
Complete the sentences with the correct form of **wake up**.

1. I _____wake_____ up early every day.

2. We _____ up early every day.

3. They _____ up early every day.

4. He _____ up early every day.

5. You _____ up early every day.

6. She _____ up early every day.

7. The dog _____ up early every day.

8. It _____ up early every day.

9. Mr. and Mrs. Ito _____ up early every day.

10. Mr. Ito _____ up early every day.

11. The teacher _____ up early every day.

12. The students _____ up early every day.

▶ **Practice 2. The simple present tense.** (Chart 3-1)
Underline the simple present verbs.

    Spiro <u>works</u> at night. He teaches auto mechanics at a school in his town. He leaves his apartment at 5:00. He catches the bus near his home. The bus comes at 5:15. It takes him 40 minutes to get to work. His classes begin at 6:30. He teaches until 10:30. He stays at school until 11:15. A friend drives him home. He gets home around midnight.

▶ **Practice 3. Form of the simple present tense.** (Chart 3-1)
Complete the sentences with the correct form of the verb in parentheses.

1. My alarm clock (*ring*) _____*rings*_____ at 5:00 every morning.

2. I (*get*) _____ out of bed slowly.

3. My husband (*make*) _____ breakfast for us.

4. He (*cook*) _____ a hot breakfast every morning.

5. We (*leave*) _____ for work at 6:00.

6. I (*drive*) _____ us to work.

7. We (*listen to*) _____ the morning news.

8. My husband and I (*work*) _____ at the same company.

9. We (*arrive*) _____ at work early.

10. Our two co-workers (*come*) _____ later.

11. They (*take*) _____ the same bus to the office.

▶ **Practice 4. Form of the simple present tense.** (Chart 3-1)
Complete the sentences with the correct form of the verb in parentheses.

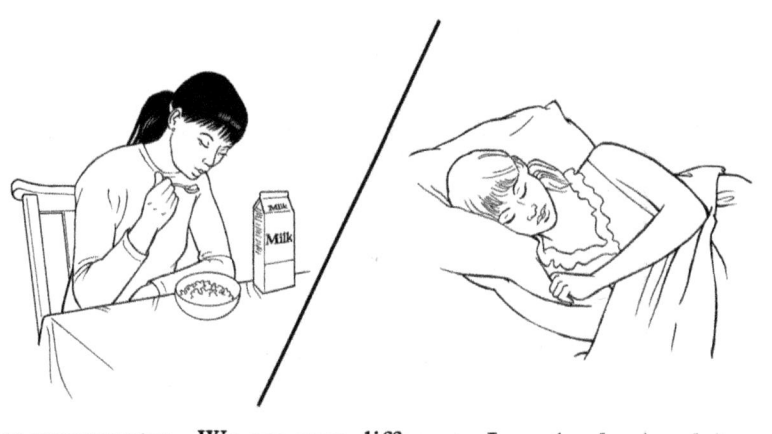

Joan and I are roommates. We are very different. Joan (*wakes / wake*) _____*wakes*_____

up early. I (*wakes / wake*) _____ up at 11:00. I (*eats / eat*) _____
                                    2                                                3
breakfast at lunchtime. Joan (*eats / eat*) _____ breakfast at 7:30. She (*leaves /*
                                                      4

*leave*) _____ for school at 8:00. I (*takes / take*) _____ evening
                  5                                                              6

classes, so I go to school at 5:00. Joan (*cooks / cook*) _____ an early dinner
                                                                    7

and (*falls / fall*) _____ asleep around 9:00. I (*eats / eat*) _____
                          8                                                          9

at midnight and (*falls / fall*) _____ asleep in the early morning. We (*sees / see*)
                                          10

_____ each other on weekends. We (*has / have*) _____ very
          11                                                                12

different lives, but we are good friends.

▶ **Practice 5. Frequency adverbs.** (Chart 3-2)
Rewrite each sentence using the given frequency adverb.

1. Olga has cream in her coffee. (*always*)

   *Olga always has cream in her coffee.*

2. I eat breakfast. (*rarely*)

   _____

3. The students buy their lunch at school. (*seldom*)

   _____

4. They bring lunch from home. (*usually*)

   _____

5. My husband and I go out to a restaurant for dinner. (*often*)

   _____

6. My husband drinks coffee with dinner. (*sometimes*)

   _____

7. We have dessert. (*never*)

   _____

▶ **Practice 6. Frequency adverbs.** (Chart 3-2)
Rewrite the sentences using an appropriate frequency adverb.

1. Beth has fish for lunch. (50% of the time)

   *Beth sometimes has fish for lunch.*

2. Roger gets up late. (10% of the time)

   _____

3. Mr. and Mrs. Phillips go to the movies on weekends. (90% of the time)

   _____

4.  I clean my apartment. (75% of the time)

_____

5.  My roommate cleans our apartment. (0% of the time)

_____

6.  The students do their homework. (100% of the time)

_____

7.  The teacher corrects papers on weekends. (50% of the time)

_____

▶ **Practice 7. Frequency adverbs.** (Chart 3-2)
Agree or disagree with the sentences about your morning activities.  If the answer is *no*, write the correct frequency adverb.

  1.  I always wake up early.                                        yes     no

  2.  I sometimes sleep late on weekends.                            yes     no

  3.  I seldom eat a hot breakfast.                                  yes     no

  4.  I often listen to the radio in the morning.                    yes     no

  5.  I usually watch TV during breakfast.                           yes     no

  6.  I rarely study English at home in the morning.                 yes     no

  7.  I never exercise in the morning.                               yes     no

▶ **Practice 8. Frequency adverbs.** (Chart 3-2)
Complete the sentences about yourself in the evening.

  1.  I always _____

  2.  I never _____

  3.  I sometimes _____

  4.  I often _____

  5.  I seldom _____

  6.  I rarely _____

► **Practice 9. Other frequency expressions.** (Chart 3-2)
Rewrite the sentences using the expressions from the box.

| | |
|---|---|
| once a day | ✓ three times a week |
| once a month | twice a month |
| once a year | twice a week |
| three times a day | twice a year |

1. I have classes on Mondays, Wednesdays, and Fridays.

   _____I have classes three times a week._____

2. I pay my phone bill on the first day of every month.

   _____

3. I exercise from 10:00 to 11:00 A.M. every day.

   _____

4. I visit my cousins in December and June every year.

   _____

5. Dr. Williams checks her email at 6:00 A.M., noon, and 10:00 P.M. every day.

   _____

6. The Browns take a long vacation in August.

   _____

7. Cyndi gives dinner parties at the beginning and end of each month.

   _____

8. Sam buys vegetables at the farmers' market on Mondays and Fridays.

   _____

► **Practice 10. Position of frequency adverbs.** (Chart 3-3)
Complete the sentences with the given frequency adverb.

1. *often*      Joan _____Ø_____ is _____*often*_____ sick.

2. *often*      Joan _____ feels _____ sick.

3. *sometimes*  Carly _____ is _____ hungry.

4. *rarely*     It _____ is _____ cold in the summer.

5. *rarely*     It _____ rains _____ in the summer.

6. *usually*    I _____ am _____ in bed at 9:00.

7. *usually*    I _____ go _____ to bed at 9:00.

8. *never*      I _____ sleep _____ late.

9. *never*      I _____ wake up _____ late.

10. *always*    I _____ am _____ up early.

► **Practice 11. Frequency adverbs.** (Charts 3-2 and 3-3)
Make sentences using the given words.

1. The teacher \ clean up the classroom \ usually

   _____*The teacher usually cleans up the classroom.*_____

2. The students \ help the teacher \ often

   _____

3. The classroom \ be clean \ always

   _____

4. The parents \ visit the class \ usually

   _____

5. The parents \ help the students with their work \ sometimes

   _____

6. The parents \ be helpful \ always

   _____

7. The classroom \ be quiet \ seldom

   _____

▶ **Practice 12. Spelling of verbs ending in -s/-es.** (Chart 3-4)
Write the correct form of the verb in the appropriate column.

| ✓ call | eat | fix | listen | talk |
|--------|-----|-----|--------|------|
| ✓ catch | finish | kiss | sleep | wish |

|      -s      |      -es      |
|-------------|--------------|
| he _____ *calls* _____ | she _____ *catches* _____ |
| he _____ | she _____ |
| he _____ | she _____ |
| he _____ | she _____ |
| he _____ | she _____ |

▶ **Practice 13. Final -s/-es.** (Charts 3-1 and 3-4)
Write the forms of the given verbs.

1. I (*teach*) _____ *teach* _____ English.

2. She (*teach*) _____ English.

3. You (*mix*) _____ the salad.

4. He (*mix*) _____ the salad.

5. Sara (*miss*) _____ her friends.

6. They (*miss*) _____ their friends.

7. I (*brush*) _____ my hair.

8. The girl (*brush*) _____ her hair.

9. She and I (*wash*) _____ the dishes.

10. He (*wash*) _____ the dishes.

11. He (*cook*) _____ dinner.

12. She (*read*) _____ magazines.

13. Richard (*watch*) _____ movies.

14. Class (*begin*) _____ early.

15. Many students (*come*) _____ late.

16. The teacher always (*come*) _____ on time.

► **Practice 14. Spelling of verbs ending in -y.** (Chart 3-5)
Complete each sentence with the correct form of **study**.

1. The students _____ *study* _____ hard.

2. One student _____ hard.

3. I _____ hard.

4. My friend _____ hard.

5. You _____ hard.

6. We _____ hard.

7. She _____ hard.

8. They _____ hard.

9. He _____ hard.

10. My friends _____ hard.

► **Practice 15. Spelling of verbs ending in -y.** (Chart 3-5)
Write the correct form of each verb in the appropriate column.

| ✓ buy | enjoy | pay | say | try |
|-------|-------|-----|-----|-----|
| ✓ cry | fly | play | study | worry |

**-ies**

he _____ *cries* _____

he _____

he _____

he _____

he _____

**-s**

she _____ *buys* _____

she _____

she _____

she _____

she _____

► **Practice 16. Simple present tense: spelling.** (Charts 3-1, 3-4, and 3-5)
Complete each sentence with the correct form of a verb from the box. You will use a verb more than one time.

| brush | close | fly | ✓ start | study |
|-------|-------|-----|---------|-------|
| call | fix | help | stop | |

1. Dr. Lee _____ *starts* _____ work at 6:00 every day.

2. Sara _____ her teeth after every meal.

3. The grocery store _____ at 11:00 every night.

4. Birds _____ south in the winter.

5. An airplane often _____ over my house.

6. I'm lucky. The bus _____ in front of my apartment building.

7. Martha is a mechanic. She _____ cars.

8. I talk to my mother on the phone every day. I _____ her, or she _____ me.

9. Inga _____ in the library every afternoon.

10. John is a teacher's assistant. He _____ the teacher with her work.

▶ **Practice 17. *Has, Does, and Goes.*** (Chart 3-6)
Make sentences about the people in the chart. Use the correct form of ***have class at***, ***do homework at***, and ***go to work at***.

|  | **Jimi** | **Marta** | **Susan** | **Paul** |
|---|---|---|---|---|
| 9:00 | class |  | homework | homework |
| 10:00 | homework | class |  |  |
| 11:00 | work | homework | class | class |
| 1:00 |  |  | work | work |
| 2:00 |  | work |  |  |

1. Jimi

   a. He ___*has class at 9:00.*___ _____

   b. He _____

   c. He _____

2. Marta

   a. She _____

   b. She _____

   c. She _____

3. Susan and Paul

   a. They _____

   b. They _____

   c. They _____

▶ **Practice 18. Simple present tense.** (Charts 3-1 → 3-6)
Complete the sentences with the words in parentheses.

Ricardo (*leave*) _____*leaves*_____ his house at 4:30 every morning.  He (*catch*)
_____ the bus near his house.  He (*get*) _____ to work at 5:00.  He
(*work*) _____ in a restaurant.  He (*fix*) _____ wonderful dishes from his
country.  Many people (*come*)_____ to the restaurant for his food.  He (*finish*)
_____ work at 3:00.  Then he (*meet, often*) _____

with students from his country and (*help*) _____ them with English.  They (*have,
usually*) _____ dinner together.  After dinner he (*go*) _____ home.
Sometimes he (*have*) _____ a snack.  He (*be, often*) _____ tired at the
end of the day, but he (*enjoy*) _____ his work and the time with the students from his
country.

▶ **Practice 19. Simple present tense.** (Charts 3-1 → 3-6)
Add **-s/-es** or **Ø** (nothing) where necessary.

Sam enjoy _*s*_ cooking.  He and his wife like _____ to have company for dinner.  They
ask _____ me to dinner about once a month.  When I arrive, his wife greet _____ me.  She
invite _____ me into the kitchen, and we talk _____ to Sam while he cook _____.  The
kitchen always smell _____ wonderful.  I get _____ very hungry when I sit _____ and talk
to Sam.  Sometimes he give _____ me a few bites of food from the pots.  When dinner is
ready, we take _____ a long time to eat it.  It taste _____ delicious.  After dinner, Sam clear
_____ the table, and his wife serve _____ dessert.  These meals are wonderful, and I always
enjoy _____ myself with Sam and his wife.

► **Practice 20.** *Need/want* (Chart 3-7)

Think about what most people *need* for life in the 21st century and what many people *want* to have. Write the words from the list in the correct column.

| | | | |
|---|---|---|---|
| ✓ air | electricity | a leather coat | a smartphone |
| diamond jewelry | an expensive house | money | a sports car |
| a digital camera | food | a place to live | water |

               ***need***                                  ***want***

     *air* _____          _____

_____          _____

_____          _____

_____          _____

_____          _____

► **Practice 21.** *Want to* and *need to* (Chart 3-7)

*Part I.* Read the story. Underline the infinitives with *want* and *need*.

    Pierre is a high school student. It is his first year of high school. He is very smart, and his classes are very easy. Pierre wants more in-class work. He wants to have more homework too. His math skills are excellent. He needs to have more difficult work. He wants to do college-level math.

    His high school says he needs to take French. But Pierre speaks fluent French because his dad is from France. He likes the French teacher, but he wants to skip the class.

    Pierre likes the social part of high school, but he wants to have more difficult academics.

*Part II.* Choose all the correct answers.

1. Pierre wants . . .

    a. to do homework.

    b. more homework.

    c. easy math.

    d. a new French teacher.

    e. a new high school.

2. Pierre wants to . . .

   a. study more.

   b. do more homework.

   c. learn advanced math.

   d. skip high school.

   e. learn to speak fluent French.

3. Pierre doesn't need . . .

   a. to do homework.

   b. to speak French.

   c. college math.

   d. easy classes.

   e. to take easy classes.

▶ **Practice 22. *Like to, need to, want to.*** (Chart 3-7)
Use the words from the list or your own words to complete the sentences. Use an infinitive (*to* + verb) in each sentence. Some words can be used more than once.

| buy | ✓ go | play | watch |
|-----|------|------|-------|
| eat | listen to | take | swim |
| cash | marry | talk to | |
| do | pay | wash | |

1. Anna is sleepy. She wants _____*to go*_____ to bed.

2. Mike wants _____ TV. There's a good program on Channel 5.

3. Do you want _____ soccer with us at the park this afternoon?

4. I need _____ Jennifer in person, not on the phone.

5. I want _____ to the bank because I need _____ a check.

6. James doesn't want _____ his homework tonight.

7. My clothes are dirty. I need _____ them.

8. I want _____ downtown today because I need _____ a new coat.

9. John loves Mary. He wants _____ her.

10. Helen needs _____ an English course.

11. Where do you want _____ lunch?

12. Do you want _____ some music on the radio?

13. Jens goes to the beach often. He likes _____ in the sea for exercise.

14. David's desk is full of overdue bills. He needs _____ his bills.

▶ **Practice 23. Simple present tense: negative.** (Charts 1-6 and 3-8)
Write the correct form of the verb. Use the negative.

|  | *have* | *eat* | *be* |
|---|---|---|---|
| 1. I | don't have | | am not |
| 2. You | | | |
| 3. He | | | |
| 4. She | | | |
| 5. It | | | |
| 6. We | | | |
| 7. They | | | |

▶ **Practice 24. Simple present tense: negative.** (Chart 3-8)
Rewrite the sentences using the negative form.

1. I have time. _____ I don't have time. _____

2. You need more time. _____

3. They eat breakfast. _____

4. Yoshi likes bananas. _____

5. Susan does her homework. _____

6. We save our money. _____

7. The printer works. _____

8. The coffee tastes good. _____

9. Mr. and Mrs. Costa drive to work. _____

► **Practice 25. Simple present tense: negative.** (Charts 1-6 and 3-8)
Use the given words to make true sentences.

1. *wear*      Cows _____ *don't wear* _____ shirts.

2. *be*        Fruit _____ *is* _____ healthy.

3. *have*      A child _____ gray hair.

4. *break*     Glass _____.

5. *grow*      Apples _____ on grass.

6. *walk*      A newborn baby _____.

7. *cry*       A newborn baby _____.

8. *fly*       Cars _____.

9. *have*      People _____ twenty fingers.

10. *help*     A doctor _____ sick people.

11. *fix*      A dentist _____ broken legs.

12. *fix*      A dentist _____ broken teeth.

13. *like*     Mice _____ cats.

14. *chase*    Cats _____ mice.

15. *be*       The sun _____ cold.

16. *rain*     It _____ a lot in London.

17. *rain*     It _____ often in Algeria.

18. *wash*     Washing machines _____ dishes.

19. *wash*     A washing machine _____ clothes.

► **Practice 26. Simple present tense: negative.** (Chart 3-8)

**Part I.** Below is information about the activities Tom, Janet, and Mark do every day. Write sentences using the given words.

|  | **Tom** | **Janet** | **Mark** |
|---|---|---|---|
| drink coffee | x | x |  |
| watch TV |  |  | x |
| walk to school | x |  |  |
| study grammar | x | x | x |
| go shopping |  | x |  |
| take the bus |  | x | x |
| skip lunch | x | x |  |
| eat dinner at home | x |  | x |
| eat dinner out* |  | x |  |

\*_eat dinner out_ = eat dinner at a restaurant.

1. (_drink coffee_) _____Tom and Janet drink coffee._____

2. (_watch TV_) _____

3. (_walk to school_) _____

4. (_study grammar_) _____

5. (_go shopping_) _____

**Part II.** What don't Tom, Janet, or Mark do every day? Write sentences using the given words.

6. (_take the bus_) _____Tom doesn't take the bus._____

7. (_watch TV_) _____

8. (_skip lunch_) _____

9. (_eat dinner at home_) _____

10. (_eat dinner out_) _____

► **Practice 27. Simple present tense: negative.** (Chart 3-8)
Complete the sentences. Use the words in parentheses. Use the simple present tense.

1. Alex (_like_) _____likes_____ tea, but he (_like, not_) _____doesn't like_____ coffee.

2. Sara (_know_) _____ Ali, but she (_know, not_) _____
   Hiroshi.

3. Pablo and Maria (_want_) _____ to stay home tonight. They (_want, not_) _____
   _____ to go to a movie.

4. Robert (*be, not*) _____ hungry. He (*want, not*) _____ a sandwich.

5. Mr. Smith (*drink, not*) _____ coffee, but Mr. Jones (*drink*) _____ twelve cups every day.

6. I (*be, not*) _____ rich. I (*have, not*) _____ a lot of money.

7. This pen (*belong, not*) _____ to me. It (*belong*) _____ to Pierre.

8. My friends (*live, not*) _____ in the dorm. They (*have*) _____ an apartment.

9. It (*be*) _____ a nice day today. It (*be, not*) _____ cold. You (*need, not*) _____ your coat.

10. Today (*be*) _____ a holiday. We (*have, not*) _____ class today.

11. Abby (*eat, not*) _____ breakfast. She (*be, not*) _____ hungry in the mornings.

12. I (*read*) _____ the newspaper. I (*watch, not*) _____ TV news.

13. My roommate (*read, not*) _____ the newspaper. She (*watch*) _____ news online.

▶ **Practice 28. Yes/no questions.** (Chart 3-9)
Make questions with the given words.

1. she \ study ___*Does she study?*___

2. they \ study _____

3. he \ know _____

4. the doctor \ know _____

5. we \ know _____

6. I \ understand _____

7. you \ understand _____

8. the manager \ understand _____

9. your roommate \ work _____

10. the car \ work _____

11. it \ work _____

12. I \ care _____

13. She \ care _____

▶ **Practice 29. Yes/no questions.** (Chart 3-9)
Below is information about four people and the activities they do. Make questions for the given answers.

|  | Tom | Roger | Renee | Lisa |
|---|---|---|---|---|
| swim | x |  |  |  |
| run |  | x |  |  |
| play soccer | x |  | x | x |
| lift weights |  | x |  | x |

1. Tom

    a. _____Does he swim?_____ Yes, he does.

    b. _____ Yes, he does.

    c. _____Does he run?_____ No, he doesn't.

    d. _____ No, he doesn't.

2. Roger

    a. _____ Yes, he does.

    b. _____ No, he doesn't.

    c. _____ Yes, he does.

3. Renee and Lisa

    a. _____ Yes, they do.

    b. _____ No, they don't.

    c. _____ No, they don't.

► **Practice 30. Short answers to yes/no questions.** (Chart 3-9)
Choose the correct response for each question.

1. Do you like fish?
   (a.) Yes, I do.          b.  Yes, I like.

2. Does your husband like fish?
   a.  Yes, he does.        b.  Yes, he likes.

3. Do you want to go out to dinner?
   a.  Yes, I want.         b.  Yes, I do.

4. Do you have a question?
   a.  Yes, I have.         b.  Yes, I do.

5. Do you need help?
   a.  Yes, I do.           b.  Yes, I need.

6. Does your friend need help?
   a.  Yes, she needs.      b.  Yes, she does.

7. Do your friends go to school?
   a.  Yes, they do.        b.  Yes, they go.

8. Does your husband teach English?
   a.  Yes, he teaches.     b.  Yes, he does.

► **Practice 31. Yes/no questions and answers.** (Chart 3-9)
Make questions.  Give short answers.

1. Ann is a doctor.  She examines children.

   _____*Does she examine*_____ adults?  No, _____*she doesn't*_____ .

2. Tom is a mechanic.  He fixes cars.

   _____ boats?  No, _____ .

3. I am a pilot.  I fly small planes.

   _____ jets?  No, _____ .

4. We are teachers.  We teach teenagers.

   _____ young children?  No, _____ .

5. My sister and I are janitors.  We clean office buildings.

   _____ schools?  No, _____ .

6. Lynn and Doug are architects.  They design houses.

   _____ offices?  No, _____ .

7. Mrs. Adams is a writer. She writes for a magazine.

_____ for a book company? No, _____.

8. I am a nurse. I work at a hospital.

_____ at a clinic? No, _____.

9. They are construction workers. They build hotels.

_____ office buildings? No, _____.

10. Mr. Smith is a musician. He plays for a symphony.

_____ for a rock band? No, _____.

▶ **Practice 32. *Be* and *do* in questions.** (Chart 3-9)
Complete the questions with a form of ***be*** or ***do***.

1. _____*Are*_____ you ready?

2. _____ the bus here?

3. _____ the bus usually come on time?

4. _____ you often ride the bus?

5. _____ the bus comfortable?

6. _____ you do your work on the bus?

7. _____ you read books on the bus?

8. _____ you enjoy the ride?

9. _____ you drive to work sometimes?

10. _____ you tired of my questions?

▶ **Practice 33. _Be_ and _do_ in questions.** (Chart 3-9)
Complete the questions and answers. Use a form of **_be_** or **_do_**.

1. A: _____*Are*_____ you sick?

   B: No, I _____ not.

   A: _____ you tired?

   B: Yes, I _____ .

   A: _____*Do*_____ you want to go to bed?

   B: No, I _____ .

2. A: _____ you know the time?

   B: Yes, I _____ . It _____ 5:55.

3. A: _____ you hungry?

   B: Yes, I _____ .

   A: _____ you want some chocolate?

   B: Sure.  Mmm.

   A: _____ you like it?

   B: No, I _____ .  I love it!!

4. A: _____ you students?

   B: Not exactly.

   A: _____ you teachers?

   B: Not exactly.

   A: What _____ you?

   B: We _____ student teachers.

5. A: _____ Mr. Jones here?

   B: No, he _____ .

   A: Where _____ he?

   B: I have no idea.

   A: _____ his wife here?

   B: No, she _____ .

   A: Where _____ she?

   B: With Mr. Jones.

6. A: Where _____ my glasses? _____ you know?

   B: No. _____ they in your purse?

   A: No, they _____.

   B: _____ they in your pocket?

   A: No.

   B: Oh, I see them! They _____ on your head.

▶ **Practice 34. Questions with *where* and *what*.** (Chart 3-10)
Complete the questions with *where* or *what*.

1. _____ does Gino live? He lives in Rome.

2. _____ does Albert work? He works at Valley Hospital.

3. _____ do the kids play after school? They play soccer.

4. _____ do you want for breakfast? I just want toast and coffee.

5. _____ do you want to sit? I want to sit at the table by the window.

6. _____ does Helene like to do for vacation? She likes to travel.

7. _____ does Helene like to go? She likes to go to Hawaii.

8. _____ do you need? I need a vacation.

▶ **Practice 35. Questions with *where* and *what*.** (Chart 3-10)
Make questions for the given answers.

1. A: *Where does David live?*

   B: In Miami. (David lives in Miami.)

2. A: _____

   B: Our email addresses. (The teacher wants our email addresses.)

3. A: _____

   B: At the Plaza Hotel. (Dr. Varma stays at the Plaza Hotel.)

4. A: _____

   B: On First Street. (I catch the bus on First Street.)

5. A: _____

   B: A new job. (Lillian needs a new job.)

6. A: _____

   B: A baby brother. (The children want a baby brother.)

7. A: _____

   B: In the park. (The construction workers eat lunch in the park.)

8. A: _____

   B: Downstairs. (Victoria and Franco are downstairs.)

9. A: _____

   B: Flowers. (Mark brings his wife flowers every week.)

10. A: _____

    B: The flight number. (I need the flight number.)

▶ **Practice 36. Questions with *where* and *what*.** (Chart 3-10)
Read the story. Make questions about Paulo for the given answers.
Use ***where*** and ***what***.

Paulo enjoys his work. He spends most of his time outdoors. He
has two jobs, one for the summer and one for the winter. In the
summer, he works in the forest. He looks for forest fires. He stays
in a lookout tower. In the winter, he works in the mountains. He
is a ski instructor. He teaches skiing to young children. He lives
in a small ski hut with other teachers. Paulo loves both jobs. He is
happy to be outdoors.

a lookout tower

1. A: _____*Where does Paulo spend most of his time?*_____

   B: Outdoors.

2. A: _____

   B: In the forest.

3. A: _____

   B: Forest fires.

4. A: _____

   B: In a lookout tower.

5. A: _____

   B: In the mountains.

6. A: _____

   B: Skiing.

7. A: _____

   B: In a small ski hut.

8. A: _____

   B: Both jobs.

a ski hut

► **Practice 37. *Where, what,* and *when* in questions.** (Charts 3-10 and 3-11)
Complete the questions with *where, what,* or *when*.

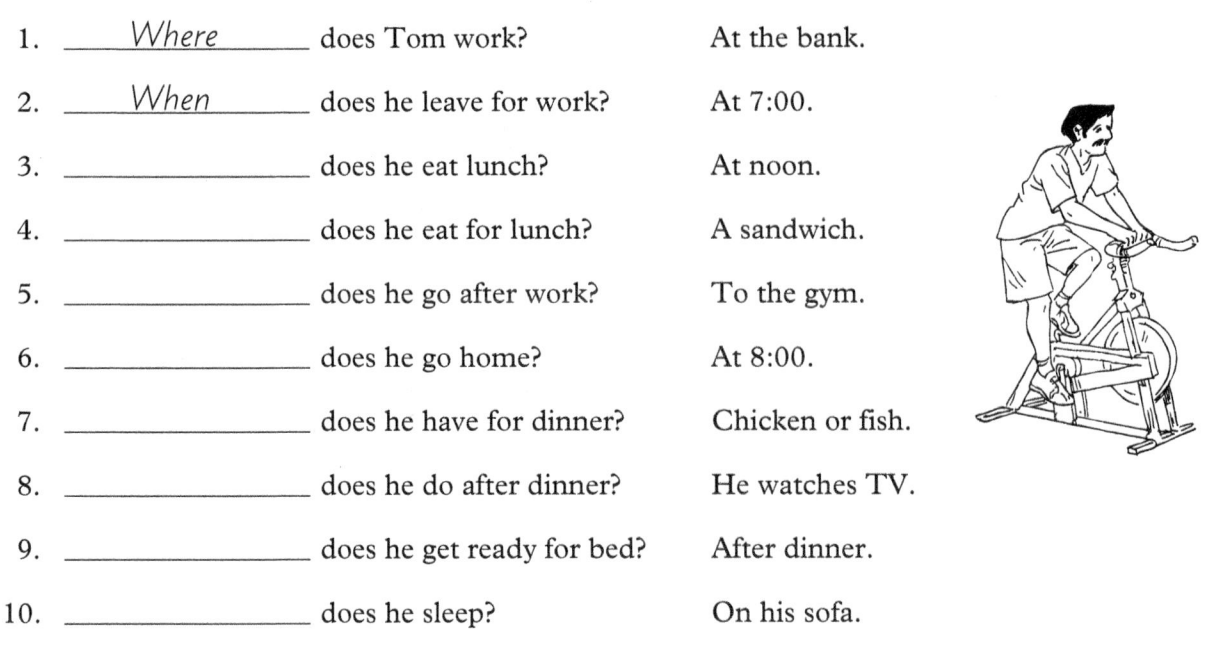

1. _____*Where*_____ does Tom work?　　　At the bank.

2. _____*When*_____ does he leave for work?　At 7:00.

3. _____ does he eat lunch?　　At noon.

4. _____ does he eat for lunch?　A sandwich.

5. _____ does he go after work?　To the gym.

6. _____ does he go home?　　At 8:00.

7. _____ does he have for dinner?　Chicken or fish.

8. _____ does he do after dinner?　He watches TV.

9. _____ does he get ready for bed?　After dinner.

10. _____ does he sleep?　　On his sofa.

► **Practice 38. Review: yes/no and information questions.** (Charts 3-9 → 3-11)
Make questions for the given answers.

1. A: _____*When do you go to bed?*_____
   B: Around 9:00. (I go to bed around 9:00.)

2. A: _____
   B: Yes, I do. (I get up early.)

3. A: _____
   B: At 5:30. (The bus comes at 5:30.)

4. A: _____
   B: Yes, it does. (The bus comes on time.)

5. A: _____
   B: At a hospital. (I work at a hospital.)

6. A: _____
   B: At 6:00. (I start work at 6:00.)

7. A: _____
   B: At 7:00. (I leave work at 7:00.)

8. A: _____
   B: Yes, I do. (I like my job.)

9. A: _____
   B: Yes, it is. (It is interesting work.)

10. A: _____
    B: Yes, I am. (I'm a doctor.)

► **Practice 39. Review: yes/no and information questions.** (Charts 3-9 → 3-11)
Read the note. Then make questions and answers about Dr. Ramos and his schedule.

1. be \ a science teacher?

   _____Is he a teacher?_____

   _____Yes, he is._____

2. what \ teach?

   _____

   _____

3. where \ teach \ chemistry?

   _____

   _____

4. when \ be \ in the chemistry lab?

   _____

   _____

5. where \ teach \ biology?

   _____

   _____

6. be \ in his office \ every day?

   _____

   _____

7. be \ in his office \ at 1:00?

   _____

   _____

8. teach \ at 8:00?

   _____

   _____

9. when \ teach?

   _____

   _____

**Dr. Ramos**

Schedule Change
My new office hours
are from 1:00 to
2:00, Monday,
Wednesday, and
Friday. I teach
biology at 9:00
and 10:00 in the
biology lab. I teach
chemistry at 12:00
in the chemistry lab.

▶ **Practice 40. Review: simple present tense.** (Chapter 3)
Complete the sentences with the correct form of the verb in parentheses. Some sentences are negative, and some are not.

1. Mario likes to talk. He (be) _____ isn't _____ quiet.

2. Janna isn't quiet. She (love) _____ loves _____ to talk.

3. Susan is a good student. She (study) _____ a lot.

4. The nurses are very busy. They (have) _____ time for lunch.

5. John's bedroom is messy. He (clean) _____ it often.

6. This soup is delicious. It (taste) _____ wonderful.

7. A new car is expensive. It (cost) _____ a lot of money.

8. Several students want to answer the question. They (know) _____ the answer.

9. Several students don't know the answer. They (want) _____ to answer the question.

10. A: Your eyes are red. You (look) _____ tired.

    B: Actually, I'm sad. I (be) _____ tired.

▶ **Practice 41. Question review.** (Chapters 2 and 3)
Make questions using the information in the note.

1. A: _____ Is Jane at home? _____
   B: No, she isn't. (Jane isn't home.)

2. A: _____
   B: At work. (She is at work.)

3. A: _____
   B: No, they aren't. (Susie and Johnny aren't home.)

4. A: _____
   B: At school. (They are at school.)

5. A: _____
   B: At 6:00. (Dinner is at 6:00.)

6. A: _____
   B: A pizza. (Jane has a pizza for dinner.)

Ron,
I'm at work. Susie and Johnny are at school. You need to pick them up. Dinner is at 6:00. I have a pizza in the fridge.*
See you soon!
Jane

*fridge = refrigerator.

► **Practice 42. Review: simple present tense.** (Chapter 3)
Choose the correct completion for each sentence.

1. Alex _____ know French.
   a. isn't      b. doesn't      c. don't

2. _____ Alex speak Russian?
   a. Is      b. Does      c. Do

3. _____ Alex from Canada?
   a. Is      b. Does      c. Do

4. When _____ you usually check your email?
   a. are      b. does      c. do

5. Anita _____ a job.
   a. no have      b. no has      c. doesn't have

6. Omar _____ his new car every Saturday.
   a. wash      b. washs      c. washes

7. Where does Tina _____ to school?
   a. go      b. goes      c. to go

8. Fumiko _____ English at this school.
   a. study      b. studies      c. studys

9. Fumiko and Omar _____ students at this school.
   a. is      b. are      c. be

10. They _____ speak the same language.
    a. aren't      b. doesn't      c. don't

# Chapter 4
## Using the Present Progressive

▶ **Practice 1. The present progressive.** (Chart 4-1)
Which sentences are true for you?

**Right now**

| | | | |
|---|---|---|---|
| 1. | The sun is shining. | yes | no |
| 2. | It is snowing outside. | yes | no |
| 3. | I am sitting at a desk. | yes | no |
| 4. | I am checking text messages. | yes | no |
| 5. | Music is playing. | yes | no |
| 6. | Friends are talking to me. | yes | no |
| 7. | People are calling me on my phone. | yes | no |

▶ **Practice 2. The present progressive.** (Chart 4-1)
Complete each sentence with *am*, *is*, or *are*.

**Right now**

1. Some students ___*are*___ waiting for the bus.

2. Their teacher _____ correcting their homework.

3. I _____ doing my homework.

4. Mark _____ doing his homework.

5. Sandra _____ shopping at the mall.

6. Her friends _____ shopping with her.

7. Mr. and Mrs. Brown _____ watching TV.

8. Their daughter _____ reading a book.

9. You _____ reading this exercise.

10. We _____ learning English.

11. My friend and I _____ learning English.

12. Dr. John _____ looking for medical information on the Internet.

13. A nurse _____ talking to a patient.

14. Several patients _____ waiting in the waiting room.

▶ **Practice 3. Spelling of -*ing*.** (Chart 4-2)
Write the -*ing* form of each verb.

1. shine _____*shining*_____     6. pay _____

2. win _____     7. study _____

3. join _____     8. get _____

4. sign _____     9. wait _____

5. fly _____     10. write _____

▶ **Practice 4. Spelling of -*ing*.** (Chart 4-2)
Write the -*ing* form of each verb.

1. dream _____*dreaming*_____     6. hit _____

2. come _____     7. hurt _____

3. look _____     8. clap _____

4. take _____     9. keep _____

5. bite _____     10. camp _____

► **Practice 5. The present progressive.** (Charts 4-1 and 4-2)
Complete each sentence with the correct form of a verb from the box. Use the present progressive.

| come | go | read | talk |
|------|-----|------|--------|
| do | kick | sit | ✓ wait |

It's 3:00 and the classroom is empty. Some students are outside. They

_____*are waiting*_____ for the city bus. A few students _____
         1                                                 2

on the ground under a tree. They _____ about their plans for the
                                           3

weekend. A girl on a bench _____ her homework. The boy next to her
                                         4

_____ a book. A few students _____ a soccer
          5                                        6

ball. The bus _____ now. The students _____
                   7                                   8

home.

► **Practice 6. The present progressive: affirmative and negative.** (Chart 4-3)

*Part I.* Tony is an engineer. Right now he is in his office. Check (✓) the activities he is doing. Make possible sentences for all the given phrases.

_✓_ meet with his manager      ____ talk on the phone

____ repair his car      ____ ride a horse

____ work at his computer      ____ buy food for dinner

1. _____*He is meeting with his manager.*_____

2. _____*He isn't repairing his car.*_____

3. _____

4. _____

5. _____

6. _____

*Part II.* Anita and Ben are nurses. Right now they are at the hospital. Check (✓) the activities they are doing. Make possible sentences for all the given phrases.

_____ talk to patients      _____ work with doctors

_____ wash cars      _____ give medicine to patients

_____ watch movies

1. _____

2. _____

3. _____

4. _____

5. _____

*Part III.* What are you doing right now? Check (✓) the activities and make true sentences for all the given phrases.

_____ listen to music      _____ study in the library

_____ sit at a desk      _____ wait for a friend

_____ work at home      _____ ride on a bus

1. _____

2. _____

3. _____

4. _____

5. _____

6. _____

▶ **Practice 7. The present progressive: affirmative and negative.** (Chart 4-3)
Use the verb in each sentence to make a true sentence.

1. I (*think*) _am thinking / am not thinking_ about my family right now.

2. I (*write*) _____ in a classroom right now.

3. I (*listen*) _____ to music right now.

4. I (*travel*) _____ in another country today.

5. A cat (*sit*) _____ beside me right now.

6. A bird (*sing*) _____ outside my window.

7. My phone (*ring*) _____ at this moment.

8. A computer printer in the room (*make*) _____ noise right now.

▶ **Practice 8. The present progressive: questions.** (Chart 4-4)
Make questions with the given words. Use the present progressive.

1. he \ study English? _____*Is he studying English?*_____

2. you \ work? _____

3. they \ leave? _____

4. she \ stay home? _____

5. we \ go to school? _____

6. the computer \ work? _____

7. it \ work? _____

8. I \ drive? _____

9. your friend \ come? _____

10. the students \ laugh? _____

11. Mr. Kim \ sleep? _____

12. Monica \ dream? _____

▶ **Practice 9. The present progressive: questions and negatives.** (Chart 4-4)
Use the verbs in parentheses to make logical questions and answers.

1. Anna is in the kitchen. (*cook, sleep*)

    A: _____*Is she sleeping*_____?

    B: No, _____*she isn't*_____. She _____*is cooking*_____.

2. Pablo is in the car. (*drive, run*)

    A: _____?

    B: No, _____. He _____.

3. Terry and Tony are in the swimming pool. (*swim, study*)

    A: _____?

    B: No, _____. They _____.

4. Mrs. Ramirez is at the supermarket. (*teach, shop*)

   A: _____?

   B: No, _____. She _____.

5. Marta is in her bedroom. (*sleep, fish*)

   A: _____?

   B: No, _____. She _____.

6. Some teenagers are in the park with their soccer ball. (*play, work*)

   A: _____?

   B: No, _____. They _____.

7. I am on a plane. (*wash dishes, read a book*)

   A: _____?

   B: No, _____. I _____.

▶ **Practice 10. The present progressive: statements, negatives, and questions.**
        (Charts 4-1 → 4-4)
Complete the sentences with the correct form of the verb ***work***.

*Part I*: Statement Forms

   1. I _____*am working*_____ right now.

   2. They _____ right now.

   3. She _____ right now.

   4. You _____ right now.

   5. He _____ right now.

*Part II:* Negative Forms

   6. I _____*am not working*_____ right now.

   7. They _____ right now.

   8. She _____ right now.

   9. You _____ right now.

   10. He _____ right now.

11. ___*Are*___ you ___*working*___ right now?

12. _____ he _____ right now?

13. _____ they _____ right now?

14. _____ we _____ right now?

15. _____ she _____ right now?

► **Practice 11. The simple present: statements, negatives, and questions.**
   (Charts 4-1 → 4-4)
Complete the sentences with the correct form of the verb **work**.

*Part I:* Statement Forms

1. I ___*work*_____ every day.

2. They _____ every day.

3. She _____ every day.

4. You _____ every day.

5. He _____ every day.

*Part II:* Negative Forms

6. I ___*do not work*_____ _____ every day.

7. They _____ every day,

8. She _____ every day.

9. You _____ every day.

10. He _____ every day.

*Part III:* Question Forms

11. ___*Do*___ you ___*work*___ every day?

12. _____ he _____ every day?

13. _____ they _____ every day?

14. _____ we _____ every day?

15. _____ she _____ every day?

▶ **Practice 12. Simple present vs. the present progressive.** (Chart 4-5)
Choose the correct completion for each sentence.

1. I send text messages         now.    (every day.)
2. I am not sending a text message    (now.)    every day.
3. I receive text messages         now.    every day.
4. I look at magazines         now.    every day.
5. I'm reading a book         now.    every day.
6. It's raining         now.    every day.
7. My kids play outside         now.    every day.
8. My kids are playing outside         now.    every day.
9. My computer isn't working         now.    every day.
10. I work at my computer         now.    every day.

▶ **Practice 13. Simple present vs. the present progressive.** (Chart 4-5)
Check (✓) the sentences that describe activities happening right now.

1. ___✓___ The phone is ringing.
2. _____ I'm talking to my sister.
3. _____ We talk two or three times a week.
4. _____ Ruth exercises in the mornings.
5. _____ She lifts weights.

6. _____ The baby is crying.
7. _____ She cries when she is hungry.
8. _____ Her mother is feeding her.
9. _____ We are listening to music.
10. _____ We listen to music in the car.

▶ **Practice 14. Simple present vs. the present progressive.** (Chart 4-5)
Complete each sentence with the correct form of the verb in parentheses.

Right now the sun (shine) _____*is shining*_____ . I (look)
1

_____ out my window at the lake. A man and a young boy
2

(fish) _____ from a small boat. A mother with a baby (sit)
3

_____ on the grass. They (play) _____ with
4                                              5

a ball. Two girls (swim) _____ near the shore. Some teenage boys
6

(jump) _____ off the dock.
7

I (*swim*) _____swim_____ in the lake every day in the summer for exercise.
                 8

In the winter, I usually (*walk*) _____ around the lake, or I (*go*)
                                        9

_____ to a gym.
        10

     Today I (*work*) _____ at home.  I usually
                              11

(*work*) _____ at home three days a week.  I (*write*)
                 12

_____ stories for children's books.  Right now I (*write*)
        13

_____ a story about a young boy and girl and a magic hat.
        14

▶ **Practice 15.  Simple present vs. the present progressive.** (Chart 4-5)
Complete each sentence with **Do**, **Does**, **Is**, or **Are**.

1. _____Do_____ you study every day?

2. _____ you working hard now?

3. _____ your class working hard now?

4. _____ you learning a lot of English?

5. _____ you memorize vocabulary every day?

6. _____ your teacher helping you now?

7. _____ your teacher help you after class?

8. _____ you do your homework every day?

9. _____ the homework take a long time?

10. _____ you understand your classmates?

11. _____ your teacher understand you?

12. _____ you ask a lot of questions?

13. _____ you studying with friends right now?

14. _____ you often study with friends?

▶ **Practice 16.  Non-action verbs.** (Chart 4-6)
Choose the correct verb form in each sentence.

1. (*Do you know* / *Are you knowing*) the names of all the students in your class?

2. Mmm.  I (*smell* / *am smelling*) something good in the oven.

3. The baby (*cries* / *is crying*) right now.  She (*is wanting* / *wants*) her mother.

4. This coffee (*is tasting / tastes*) wonderful. I (*like / am liking*) strong coffee.

5. The cat and dog (*are running / run*) outside right now. The dog (*likes / is liking*) the cat, but the cat (*is hating / hates*) the dog.

▶ **Practice 17. Non-action verbs.** (Chart 4-6)
Complete each sentence with the correct form of the verb in parentheses.

1. A: Mmm. This bread (*taste*) _____*tastes*_____ delicious.

   B: Thank you. I (*think*) _____ it has honey in it.

2. A: What (*Jan, want*) _____ for her birthday?

   B: Well, she (*need*) _____ a winter coat, but she (*want*)
   _____ leather boots.

3. A: Shhh. (*you, hear*) _____ a siren?

   B: I (*hear*) _____ it, but I (*see, not*)
   _____ it.

4. A: Jackie (*love*) _____ Carl.

   B: What? I (*believe, not*) _____ you. Carl (*love*)
   _____ me!

▶ **Practice 18. *See, look at, watch, hear,* and *listen to*.** (Chart 4-7)
Choose the correct sentence in each pair.

1. a. I am hearing the neighbor's TV. It's very loud.
   (b.) I hear the neighbor's TV. It's very loud.

2. a. Look! I see a deer.
   b. Look! I am seeing a deer.

3. a. Annette isn't listening to me right now.
   b. Annette doesn't listen to me right now.

4. a. Shhh. I watch a movie.
   b. Shhh. I'm watching a movie.

a deer

5. a. I look at the clock. We are late.
   b. I'm looking at the clock. We are late.

6. a. Mary, what are you looking at?
   b. Mary, what do you look at?

7. a. Do you hear that noise? It sounds like an earthquake.
   b. Are you hearing that noise? It sounds like an earthquake.

8. a. I am listening to the radio at night. It helps me fall asleep.
   b. I listen to the radio at night. It helps me fall asleep.

9. a. I hear my cell phone. I need to answer it right now.
   b. I am hearing my cell phone. I need to answer it right now.

▶ **Practice 19. See, look at, watch, hear, and listen to.** (Chart 4-7)
Complete each sentence with the correct form of the verb in parentheses.

Andy is sitting in his living room right now. He

(*watch*) _____is watching_____ a football game on TV. His
               1

favorite team (*play*) _____. He
                              2

(*listen, also*) _____ to the game
                        3

on the radio and (*look*) _____
                                4

at sports information in the newspaper. He

(*wear*) _____
              5

headphones. His wife (*talk*) _____ to him. She (*tell*)
                                     6

_____ him her plans for the day. He (*listen, not*)
        7

_____ because he (*hear, not*) _____
        8                                                          9

her. Suddenly, she turns off the TV. Now Andy (*listen*) _____
                                                                        10

very carefully.

▶ **Practice 20. See, look at, watch, hear, and listen to.** (Chart 4-7)
Choose the correct verb in each sentence.

1. In the evenings, I like to sit in front of the TV and (*watch* / *see*) old movies.

2. The neighbors are having a party. I (*hear* / *listen to*) a lot of loud noise.

3. Shhh. I (*hear* / *listen to*) something. Is someone outside?

4. I love rock music. When I'm at home, I put on my headphones, sit down, and
   (*hear* / *listen to*) rock music.

5. A: Let's go shopping. I want to (*look at* / *watch*) clothes.

   B: Okay. You can (*look at* / *see*) clothes. I want to sit on a bench and (*see* / *watch*) the
      people at the mall.

6. A: Look out the window. (*Do you see / Do you watch*) the storm clouds?

   B: I (*see / look at*) several dark rain clouds.

▶ **Practice 21. Review.** (Charts 4-6 and 4-7)
Write true sentences using the given verbs.

Right now I. . .

1. (*look at*) _____.

2. (*see*) _____.

3. (*hear*) _____.

4. (*listen to*) _____.

5. (*watch*) _____.

6. (*want*) _____.

7. (*need*) _____.

▶ **Practice 22. *Think about* and *think that*.** (Chart 4-8)
Choose the correct sentence in each pair.

1. a. You are very quiet. What do you think about?
   (b.) You are very quiet. What are you thinking about?

2. a. I am thinking about my plans for today.
   b. I think about my plans for today.

3. a. I am thinking that grammar is difficult.
   b. I think that grammar is difficult.

4. a. What are you thinking? Does this shirt look okay?
   b. What do you think? Does this shirt look okay?

5. a. Joe, do you think that sports stars get too much money?
   b. Joe, are you thinking that sports stars get too much money?

▶ **Practice 23. *Think about* and *think that*.** (Chart 4-8)
Complete each sentence with the correct form of ***think that*** or ***think about***.

1. A: What _____ *are* _____ you _____ *thinking about* _____
      right now?

   B: I _____ my family. I miss them.

   A: You have a nice family. I _____ you are lucky.

2. A: Some people _____ English is an easy language.

   B: I (*not*) _____ it is easy to learn.  I

   _____ it is difficult.

3. A: I have a new game.  I _____ an animal.  It

   is very long and sometimes dangerous.  Do you know the animal?  Can you guess?

   B: _____ you _____ a snake?

   A: Yes!

   B: I _____ snakes make nice pets, but many people are

   afraid of them.

   A: I'm afraid of them.  I _____ they are scary.

▶ **Practice 24. Verb review.** (Chapters 3 and 4)
   Complete each sentence with the correct form of the verb in parentheses.

   1. Tony's family (*eat*) _____*eats*_____ dinner at the same time every day.
   During dinner, the phone sometimes (*ring*) _____.

      Tony's mother (*answer, not*) _____ it.  She
      (*want, not*) _____ her teenagers to talk on the phone
      during dinner.  She (*believe*) _____ dinner is an important
      time for the family.

   2. Olga Burns is a pilot for an airline company in Alaska.  She (*fly*) _____
      almost every day.  Today she (*fly*) _____ from Juneau to
      Anchorage.

   3. A: Excuse me.  (*you, wait*) _____ for the downtown bus?

      B: Yes, I (*be*) _____.

      A: What time (*the bus, stop*) _____ here?

      B: Ten thirty-five.

      A: (*be, usually, it*) _____ on time?

      B: Yes.  It (*come, rarely*) _____ late.

   4. A: What (*your teacher, do, usually*) _____
      at lunchtime every day?

      B: I (*think*) _____ she (*correct*) _____
      papers in the classroom and (*have*) _____ lunch.

      A: What (*she, do*) _____ right now?

      B: She (*talk*) _____ to a student.

5. A: (*you, know*) _____ the capital of Australia?

   B: I (*believe*) _____ it (*be*) _____ Vienna.

   A: Not Austria. Australia!

   B: Oh. Wait a minute. Let me think. I (*know*) _____. It's Canberra.

▶ **Practice 25. Verb review.** (Chapters 3 and 4)
Complete each sentence with the word or words in parentheses. Use the simple present or the present progressive. Use an infinitive where necessary.

The Lind family is at home. It is evening. Jens (*sit*) _____ on the
                                                                    1
couch. He (*look at*) _____ a weather report on his computer. Brita
                            2
(*work*) _____ at her desk. She (*study*) _____
                3                                                                4
and (*listen to*) _____ music. Jens (*hear*) _____ the
                        5                                                        6
music, but he (*listen to, not*) _____ it right now. He (*think about*)
                                        7
_____ the weather report.
        8
   Brita (*memorize*) _____ chemistry formulas. She (*like*)
                                9
_____ chemistry. She (*think*) _____ that chemistry is
        10                                                            11
easy. She (*understand*) _____ it. Chemistry (*be*) _____
                                12                                                            13
her favorite course. She (*like, not*) _____ history.
                                                14

$$2H_2 + O_2 \rightarrow 2H_2O$$
a chemistry formula

Mr. Lind is in the kitchen. He (*cook*) _____ 15 dinner. He (*cook*) _____ 16 three or four times a week. He (*cut*) _____ 17 vegetables for a salad. Steam (*rise*) _____ 18 from a pot on the stove.

Mrs. Lind (*stand*) _____ 19 near the front door. She (*take off*) _____ 20 her jacket. She (*wear*) _____ 21 exercise clothes because she (*exercise, usually*) _____ 22 after work. She (*think about*) _____ 23 dinner. She (*be*) _____ 24 very hungry, and the food (*smell*) _____ 25 good. After dinner, she (*want*) _____ 26 (*watch*) _____ 27 a TV show with her family. Their favorite show (*be*) _____ 28 on tonight. She (*need*) _____ 29 (*go*) _____ 30 to bed afterwards because she has a busy day at work tomorrow.

In the corner of the living room, a mouse (*eat*) _____ 31 a piece of cheese. Their cat (*be*) _____ 32 nearby, but she (*sleep*) _____ 33. She (*dream about*) _____ 34 a mouse.

Nine-year-old Axel is in the middle of the living room. He (*play*) _____ 35 with a toy train. He (*see, not*) _____ 36 the mouse because he (*look at*) _____ 37 his train. Their bird (*sing*) _____ 38. Axel (*listen to, not*) _____ 39 it. But Mrs. Lind (*hear*) _____ 40 the bird. She (*like*) _____ 41 (*listen to*) _____ 42 it sing.

# Chapter 5

## Talking About the Present

▶ **Practice 1. Using *it* with time and dates.** (Chart 5-1)
Read the email message. Make questions for the answers. Begin each question with ***What***.

| To: | Brooks, Jim |
| --- | --- |
| From: | Hernandez, Sue |
| Date: | Tue 3/5/2014 6:00 A.M. |
| Subject: | See you soon |

Hi Jim,

It's 6:00 Tuesday morning in Tokyo. I'm sitting in my hotel room. I'm waiting for the airport bus. Great trip. Miss you—see you tomorrow!

Sue

1. _____*What day is it?*_____ It's Tuesday.

2. _____ It's 6:00 A.M.

3. _____ It's March 5th.

4. _____ It's 2014.

5. _____ It's March.

6. _____ It's six o'clock.

7. _____ It's the 5th of March.

▶ **Practice 2. Using *it* with time and dates.** (Chart 5-1)
Choose the correct response to each question.

1. What's the date today?
   a. It's April 1.    b. It's Monday.

2. What day is it?
   a. It's February 2.    b. It's Friday.

3. What month is it?
   a. It's January 2nd.    b. It's December.

4. What time is it?
   a. It's 9:55.          b. It's 9:55 o'clock.

5. What's the date today?
   a. It's Monday.        b. It's the 2nd of May.

▶ **Practice 3. Prepositions of time.** (Chart 5-2)
Complete each sentence with the correct preposition.

1. I wake up . . .

   a. ___in___ the morning.

   b. _____ 7:00.

2. My husband goes to work . . .

   a. _____ 1:00 P.M.

   b. _____ the afternoon.

   c. _____ Mondays, Wednesdays, and Thursdays.

3. I work . . .

   a. _____ the evening.

   b. _____ night.

   c. _____ 5:00 _____ midnight.

   d. _____ Saturday.

   e. _____ Saturdays.

4. My husband was born . . .

   a. _____ December.

   b. _____ December 26.

   c. _____ the afternoon.

   d. _____ 1:00 _____ the afternoon.

   e. _____ December 26, 1989.

   f. _____ 1989.

▶ **Practice 4. Prepositions of time.** (Chart 5-2)
Complete each sentence with *in*, *on*, *at*, *from*, or *to*.

1.  I have English class ____*in*____ the morning.

2.  My first class begins _____ 9:00 A.M.

3.  The class goes _____ 9:00 _____ 9:55.

4.  I don't have class _____ Fridays.

5.  My math class meets _____ the evenings.

6.  I don't like to study _____ night.

7.  I prefer to study _____ the afternoon.

8.  There is no class _____ May 1st.

9.  Summer vacation goes _____ June _____ September.

▶ **Practice 5. Talking about the weather.** (Chart 5-3)
Use the weather information in the box.

| Moscow | 0°C | 32°F | partly cloudy, snow |
| Sydney | 24°C | 75°F | clear, dry |
| Seoul | 5°C | 41°F | heavy rain, strong winds |
| Cairo | 38°C | 100°F | clear, dry |

*Part I.* Make questions for the given answers.

1.  ____*How's the weather / What's the weather like in Cairo?*____ It's hot.

2.  _____ It's warm.

3.  _____ It's stormy.

4.  _____ It's beautiful.

5.  _____ It's freezing.

*Part II.* Circle *yes* or *no*.

6.  It is chilly in Moscow.          (yes)     no

7.  It is wet in Cairo.              yes     no

8.  It is freezing in Seoul.         yes     no

9.  It is humid in Sydney.           yes     no

10. It is nice in Sydney.            yes     no

11. It is clear in Seoul.            yes     no

► **Practice 6. Asking about the weather.** (Charts 5-1 and 5-3)
Complete the questions with words from the box.

| how's | like | temperature | the weather |
|---|---|---|---|

1. What's the weather _____ in your hometown?

2. _____ the weather in your hometown?

3. What's the average _____ in the summer?

4. What's the average _____ in the winter?

5. How's _____ in Singapore right now?

► **Practice 7. Questions: time and weather.** (Charts 5-1 and 5-3)
Choose the correct completion for each sentence.

1. What ____ the weather like today?
   a. is it          b. is

2. What month ____?
   a. is it          b. is

3. What ____ the date today?
   a. is it          b. is

4. What day ____?
   a. is it          b. is

5. What time ____?
   a. is it          b. is

6. How ____ the weather?
   a. is it          b. is

7. What year ____?
   a. is it          b. is

► **Practice 8. *There + be.*** (Chart 5-4)
Look around the room you are in. Choose the correct verb, and then circle *yes* or *no*.

1. There (*is* / *are*) one student in this room.          yes          no
2. There (*is* / *are*) two students in this room.          yes          no
3. There (*is* / *are*) a desk.          yes          no
4. There (*is* / *are*) one door.          yes          no
5. There (*is* / *are*) two doors.          yes          no
6. There (*is* / *are*) three windows.          yes          no
7. There (*is* / *are*) a computer.          yes          no

8. There (*is / are*) a TV.                    yes    no

9. There (*is / are*) chairs.                   yes    no

▶ **Practice 9. *There + be*.** (Chart 5-4)
Make sentences about the picture using the given words.

1. (*two chairs*)    ___There are two chairs.___

2. (*one couch*)    _____

3. (*one table*)    _____

4. (*four books*)    _____

5. (*one lamp*)    _____

6. (*two pillows*)    _____

▶ **Practice 10. *There + be*: yes/no questions.** (Chart 5-5)
Think about your bedroom. Circle the correct form of *be*. Then write short answers.

1. (*Is* / *Are*)    there a bed in your bedroom?          ___Yes, there is. / No, there isn't.___

2. (*Is / Are*)    there a window in your bedroom?        _____

3. (*Is / Are*)    there four windows in your bedroom?    _____

4. (*Is / Are*)    there a pillow on your bed?            _____

5. (*Is / Are*)    there six pillows on your bed?         _____

6. (*Is / Are*)    there sheets on your bed?              _____

7. (*Is / Are*)    there a TV in your bedroom?            _____

8. (*Is / Are*)    there two closets in your bedroom?     _____

9. (*Is / Are*)    there a mirror in your bedroom?        _____

► **Practice 11. *There + be*: yes/no questions.** (Chart 5-5)
You are new to a town. Make questions about the places in parentheses. Begin with ***Is there***
or ***Are there***.

1. (*a subway*) _____Is there a subway?_____

2. (*a bus station*) _____

3. (*fast-food restaurants*) _____

4. (*movie theaters*) _____

5. (*a park*) _____

6. (*places to exercise*) _____

7. (*a visitor information office*) _____

► **Practice 12. *There + be*: questions with *how many*.** (Chart 5-6)
Choose the correct noun in each question.

1. How many (*boy / boys*) are there in the world?

2. How many (*girl / girls*) are there in the world?

3. How many (*car / cars*) are there in the world?

4. How many (*word / words*) are there in a dictionary?

5. How many (*minute / minutes*) are there in a day?

6. How many (*second / seconds*) are there in a day?

7. How many (*star / stars*) are there in the sky?

8. How many (*snowflake / snowflakes*) are there in a snowball?

a snowflake

► **Practice 13. *There + be*: questions with how many.** (Chart 5-6)
Complete each question with a word or phrase from the box. Begin with ***How many***.

| | | |
|---|---|---|
| colors | countries | main languages |
| ✓ continents | letters | states |

1. _____How many continents are there_____ in the world?  There are seven.

2. _____ in Australia?  There are six.

3. _____ on the Thai flag?  There are three.

4. _____ in North America?  There are three.

5. _____ in the English alphabet?  There are twenty-six.

6. _____ in Canada?  There are two:  French and English.

► **Practice 14. *There + be*: questions with *how many*.** (Chart 5-6)
Make questions using the given words and ***How many***. Then give short answers.

1. sentence \ in this exercise

   _____How many sentences are there in this exercise?_____  _____There are seven._____

2. exercise \ in this chapter

   _____  _____

3. page \ in your dictionary

   _____  _____

4. student \ in your class

   _____  _____

5. male \ in your class

   _____  _____

6. female \ in your class

   _____  _____

7. teacher \ at your school

   _____  _____

► **Practice 15. Prepositions of place.** (Chart 5-7)
Complete each sentence with the correct preposition: *in, on,* or *at*.

1. Marco lives ____*in*____ Italy.

2. Tina lives _____ Vancouver, Canada.

3. Tina works _____ Robson Street.

4. Margaret lives _____ 6456 1st Street.

5. Margaret lives _____ 1st Street.

6. Jeffrey lives _____ Australia.

7. Jeffrey works _____ 2nd Street.

8. Jeffrey works _____ 5725 2nd Street.

► **Practice 16. At or in.** (Chart 5-7)
Complete the sentences with *at* or *in*.

1. Renata is sleeping. She is _____ bed _____ her bedroom.

2. Jack is very sick. He is a patient. He is _____ the hospital.

3. Mrs. Nelson is a university professor. Her students are _____ class. They are sitting _____ the classroom.

4. Everyone in class is listening to the teacher. They are _____ school right now.

5. Kellen is absent today. He is _____ home.

6. His wife is not _____ home. She is _____ work.

7. Your shoes are _____ the hall.

8. Extra chairs are _____ the kitchen.

9. Carlos is a thief. He is _____ jail.

10. His father is also a thief. He is _____ prison.

► **Practice 17. At or in.** (Chart 5-7)
Complete the sentences with *at* or *in*.

Last week, Ben was . . .

1. ____*at*____ home.

2. _____ school for a meeting.

3. _____ work.

4. _____ the bedroom.

5. _____ bed.

6. _____ the hospital visiting a friend.

7. _____ the post office.

8. _____ class.

9. _____ his hometown of Mountain View.

10. on the phone with someone _____ jail.

▶ **Practice 18. *At* or *in*.** (Chart 5-7)
Complete the sentences about the Johnson family. Use ***at*** or ***in***.

It's 10:00 A.M. Where is everyone?

1. Mr. Johnson is ___*in*___ his office ___*at*___ work.

2. Mrs. Johnson is _____ the library with her first-grade class.

3. Joe is _____ class _____ school.

4. Beth is sick _____ home _____ bed.

5. Rita is on vacation _____ Hawaii.

6. Bob is _____ work. He is working _____ a bookstore.

7. Grandma Johnson is _____ the hospital. She is very sick.

▶ **Practice 19. Prepositions of place.** (Chart 5-8)
Complete each sentence with a preposition. There may be more than one possible completion.

1. The rabbit is _____*in / inside*_____ the hat.

2. The rabbit is _____ the hat.

3. The rabbit is _____ the hat.

4. The rabbit is _____ the hat.

5. The rabbit is _____ the hat.

6. The rabbit is _____ the hat.

7. The rabbit is _____ the hat.

8. The rabbit is _____ the hats.

▶ **Practice 20. Prepositions of place.** (Chart 5-8)
Answer the questions with prepositional expressions.

1. Where are your legs?

   _____Under my desk. / On the floor. / Etc._____

2. Where are your feet?

   _____

3. Where is your left hand?

   _____

4. Where is your right hand?

   _____

5. Where is your workbook?

   _____

6. Where is your pen or pencil?

   _____

▶ **Practice 21. _Would like._** (Chart 5-9)
Complete each sentence with the correct form of **_would like_**.

1. I _____would like_____ to leave.

2. You _____ to leave.

3. He _____ to leave.

4. She _____ to leave.

5. The cat _____ to leave.

6. Mrs. Jones _____ to leave.

7. We _____ to leave.

8. They _____ to leave.

9. The students _____ to leave.

10. Their teacher _____ to leave.

11. My friend _____ to leave.

12. My parents _____ to leave.

▶ **Practice 22. _Would like_ vs. _like._** (Chart 5-10)
Decide the meaning of each sentence. Choose **want** or **like**.

| | | |
|---|---|---|
| 1. I would like a cup of coffee. | (want) | like |
| 2. I enjoy coffee in the morning. | want | like |
| 3. My husband enjoys tea. | wants | likes |
| 4. He would like to try decaffeinated tea. | wants | likes |
| 5. I don't enjoy decaffeinated coffee. | want | like |
| 6. We would like some coffee now. | want | like |

▶ **Practice 23. _Would like_ vs. _like._** (Chart 5-10)
Rewrite the sentences with **_would like_** where possible.

1. Mark wants to have a large family. _____Mark would like to have a large family._____

2. He enjoys children. _____(no change)_____

3. Children enjoy Mark. _____

4. Mark wants to get married this year. _____

5. He wants a pet this year too. _____

6. He enjoys cats, dogs, and birds. _____

7. What does he want first? _____

▶ **Practice 24. Review.** (Chapters 4 and 5)

*Part I.* Answer the questions. Use vocabulary from the box.

| | | |
|---|---|---|
| sleep | a bed | a dream |
| (be) in love | a blanket | a head |
| dream | a clock | a pillow |
| dream about (someone/something) | | |

1. What is Mary doing?
2. What is John doing?
3. What are Mary and John doing?
4. What do you see in the picture?
5. Is Mary in her bedroom?

6. Is John in class? Where is he?
7. Is John standing or lying down?
8. Is Mary dreaming?
9. Are Mary and John dreaming about each other?
10. Are John and Mary in love?

*Part II.* Complete the sentences.

11. John and Mary _____ sleeping. They are _____ bed.

12. John _____ dreaming _____ Mary. Mary _____ dreaming

    _____ John. They ____ _____ dreaming _____ each other.

13. Mary's head is _____ a pillow.

14. John and Mary _____ in the living room.

15. They _____ asleep. They _____ awake.

16. John and Mary love each other. They are _____ love.

17. They would like _____ get married someday.

▶ **Practice 25. Review.** (Chapter 5)
Choose the correct completion for each sentence.

1. There _____ in our classroom.
   a. is twenty desks   b. are twenty desks   c. is twenty desk   d. are twenty desk

2. What _____ today?
   a. day is it   b. is day   c. day it   d. is it day

3. How many _____ there in your class?
   a. students are     b. student is     c. students     d. student

4. Dr. Smith is tired. She _____ to go home and sleep now.
   a. likes     b. would likes     c. would like     d. like

5. There _____ in a minute.
   a. is sixty second     b. are sixty second     c. is sixty seconds     d. are sixty seconds

6. The students _____ finish their work.
   a. needs to     b. need     c. needs     d. need to

7. What _____ the weather like in Bangkok?
   a. is     b. does     c. do     d. are

8. Philip lives _____ Dexter Avenue.
   a. in     b. at     c. on     d. next

9. Jason likes to sit _____ the room.
   a. in middle of     b. in the middle of     c. middle of     d. in middle

10. How _____ in Tokyo?
    a. the weather     b. is the weather     c. weather     d. is weather

11. Pam works _____ Tenth Avenue.
    a. next     b. at     c. in     d. on

12. I'm getting my hair cut _____ 2:45.
    a. in     b. on     c. from     d. at

13. The weather in my country is very hot _____ August.
    a. from     b. in     c. at     d. on

# Chapter 6
## Nouns and Pronouns

▶ **Practice 1. Identifying nouns.** (Chart 6-1)
Check (✓) the words that are nouns. Remember, nouns are *persons*, *places*, or *things*.

1. _✓_ father
2. ____ happy
3. ____ choose
4. ____ young
5. ____ snacks
6. ____ radio
7. ____ Beijing
8. ____ Mary
9. ____ hospital
10. ____ eat

Beijing *
CHINA

▶ **Practice 2. Identifying nouns.** (Chart 6-1)
Read the message. <u>Underline</u> the nouns.

Mike,
I am shopping at the store. On my list I have eggs, bananas, rice, and tea. What else do you want? Call me on my cell.*

Judy

▶ **Practice 3. Identifying subjects.** (Chart 6-1)
<u>Underline</u> the subjects.

1. <u>The weather</u> is very cold today.
2. Snow is falling.
3. The sun isn't shining.

---

*cell* = cell phone.

4. The children and their parents are playing outside in the snow.

5. Some people are throwing snowballs.

6. Teenagers are building a huge snowman.

▶ **Practice 4. Identifying objects.** (Chart 6-1)
Read the sentences and answer the questions. Then write the object of each sentence.
Remember:

1. Objects come after the verb.

2. Objects are **nouns**.

a worm

1. Birds eat worms. What do birds eat? _____ *Worms.* _____ OBJECT: _____ *Worms.* _____

2. Fish swim. What do fish do? _____ *They swim.* _____
   OBJECT: _____ *Ø* _____

3. Doctors help patients. Who do doctors help? _____
   OBJECT: _____

4. Babies drink milk. What do babies drink? _____
   OBJECT: _____

5. Babies drink several times a day. What do babies do? _____
   OBJECT: _____

6. Babies watch their mothers carefully.

   Who do babies watch? _____

   OBJECT: _____

▶ **Practice 5. Identifying objects.** (Chart 6-1)
Check (✓) the sentences that have objects of verbs. Underline the objects.

1. a. _✓_ I read the <u>newspaper</u>.
   b. ____ I read every morning.
   c. _✓_ I read the <u>newspaper</u> every morning.

2. a. ____ The children play every day.
   b. ____ The children play at the park.
   c. ____ The children play soccer.

3. a. ____ My father cooks several times a week.
   b. ____ My father cooks eggs.
   c. ____ My father cooks eggs several times a week.

4. a. ＿＿＿ Dogs chew bones.

   b. ＿＿＿ Dogs chew furniture.

   c. ＿＿＿ Dogs chew with their sharp teeth.

5. a. ＿＿＿ We are eating.

   b. ＿＿＿ We are eating lunch.

6. a. ＿＿＿ Jan teaches English.

   b. ＿＿＿ Jan teaches at a private college.

   c. ＿＿＿ Jan teaches three days a week.

   d. ＿＿＿ Jan teaches English three days a week.

7. a. ＿＿＿ Joe is staying with his cousins.

   b. ＿＿＿ Joe is staying with his cousins for one week.

8. a. ＿＿＿ Pedro helps with the housework.

   b. ＿＿＿ Pedro helps Maria with the housework.

a bone

▶ **Practice 6. Prepositions.** (Chart 6-2)
Check (✓) the prepositional phrases. Then underline the noun that is the object of each preposition. Remember, prepositions are words like *in, on, at, from, to, with, by*, etc.

1. ＿＿＿ every day        6. ＿＿＿ some trees and flowers

2. ＿✓＿ in the morning      7. ＿＿＿ across the street

3. ＿＿＿ with her children     8. ＿＿＿ three times a week

4. ＿＿＿ on the table        9.       at work

5. ＿＿＿ is paying money     10. ＿＿＿ near my house

▶ **Practice 7. Identifying objects of prepositions.** (Chart 6-2)
Check (✓) the sentences that have objects of prepositions. Underline the objects.

1. a. ＿✓＿ Samira works at a bakery.

   b. ＿＿＿ Samira works very hard.

2. a. ＿＿＿ I have chocolate in my backpack.

   b. ＿＿＿ I have chocolate a few times a week.

   c. ＿＿＿ I have chocolate for a snack.

3. a. ＿＿＿ Jake and Monica study together.

   b. ＿＿＿ Jake and Monica study in the library.

   c. ＿＿＿ Jake and Monica study every evening.

   d. ＿＿＿ Jake and Monica study at night.

4. a. ＿＿＿ The teacher is speaking with her students.

   b. ＿＿＿ The teacher is speaking quickly.

   c. ＿＿＿ The teacher is speaking in the classroom.

▶ **Practice 8. Identifying nouns and adjectives.** (Chart 6-3)
Write the words from the box in the correct column.

| ✓ bright | easy | job | poor | tree |
| ✓ car | food | leg | quiet | wet |
| chair | fresh | nervous | rain | |

nervous

| Nouns | Adjectives |
|-------|-----------|
| car | bright |
| _____ | _____ |
| _____ | _____ |
| _____ | _____ |
| _____ | _____ |
| _____ | _____ |
| _____ | _____ |

▶ **Practice 9. Nouns and adjectives.** (Chart 6-3)
Write the adjective that has the opposite meaning.

1. happy          sad

2. new          _____

3. soft          _____

4. beautiful          _____

5. young          _____

6. boring          _____

7. fast          _____

8. tall          _____

9. easy          _____

10. noisy          _____

► **Practice 10. Identifying nouns and adjectives.** (Charts 6-1 and 6-3)
Write "N" over the nouns and "A" over the adjectives.

         N           A    N

1. My sister lives in a new apartment.

2. It is very bright.

3. The rooms are large and have tall ceilings.

4. Her building is next to a Japanese restaurant.

5. I love food from other countries.

6. Mexican food is spicy and delicious.

7. There is a wonderful café in my neighborhood.

8. My neighbors like to meet there for coffee.

► **Practice 11. Using adjectives.** (Chart 6-3)
Choose two to four adjectives to describe the given nouns. Adjectives may be used more than once. Use Chart 6-3, p. 164, in the Student Book for ideas.

1. _____smart,_____ students

2. _____ tests

3. _____ neighbors

4. _____ fruit

► **Practice 12. Adjectives.** (Chart 6-3)
Some nationality adjectives are listed below. Write the country next to each adjective.

| **Nationality** | **Country** |
|---|---|
| 1. American | _____the United States (America)_____ |
| 2. Australian | _____ |
| 3. Canadian | _____ |
| 4. Chinese | _____ |
| 5. Egyptian | _____ |
| 6. Indian | _____ |
| 7. Indonesian | _____ |
| 8. Italian | _____ |
| 9. Japanese | _____ |

10. Korean           _____

11. Malaysian        _____

12. Mexican          _____

13. Russian          _____

14. Saudi Arabian    _____

Write two more nationalities and countries.

_____  _____

_____  _____

▶ **Practice 13. Using adjectives.** (Chart 6-3)
Answer the questions. Use nationality adjectives in your answers.

1. What are your favorite ethnic foods? (Ethnic food is food from another country.)

   _____

2. What kind of foreign films do you enjoy? (Foreign films are movies from other countries.)

   _____

3. What cultures do you know something about?

   _____

▶ **Practice 14. Subject and object pronouns.** (Chart 6-4)
Complete the sentences. Use pronouns (**I**, **me**, **he**, **him**, etc.).

1. Susan knows Thomas. _____*She*_____ knows _____*him*_____ well.

2. Thomas knows Susan. _____ knows _____ well.

3. Susan helps her co-workers. _____ helps _____ a lot.

4. Thomas helps his co-workers. _____ helps _____ a lot.

5. Susan and Thomas help their co-workers. _____ help _____ a lot.

6. Thomas and Susan rarely see Mr. Jones. _____ don't know _____ well.

7. Thomas and Susan rarely see Mrs. Jones. _____ don't know _____ well.

8. Susan and Thomas don't talk to their neighbors very much. _____ don't know _____ well.

9. The neighbors don't talk to Susan and Thomas very much. _____ don't know _____ well.

▶ **Practice 15. Subject and object pronouns.** (Chart 6-4)
Complete each sentence with the correct subject or object pronoun.

1. Grandpa John is in the picture. Do you see _____ *him* _____?

2. Grandma Ella is in the picture. Do you see _____?

3. My son and daughter are in the picture. Do you see _____?

4. Your brother is in the picture. Do you see _____?

5. I am in the picture. Do you see _____?

6. Your brother and I are in the picture. Do you see _____?

7. King, our dog, is in the picture. Do you see _____?

8. Queen, our cat, is in the picture. Do you see _____?

9. I don't see your sister. Where is _____?

10. I don't see King. Where is _____?

11. I don't see the dog and cat. Where are _____?

12. I don't see my son. Where is _____?

13. I don't see my brother and you. Where are _____?

14. I don't see you. Where are _____?

▶ **Practice 16. Object pronouns.** (Chart 6-4)
Complete each sentence with the correct pronoun (*her, him, it, them*).

1. A: When do you take your children to school?

   B: I take _____ *them* _____ at 8:30.

2. A: When do you have breakfast?

   B: I have _____ at 9:00.

3. A: When do you call your friends?

   B: I call _____ in the evening.

4.  A: When do you call your husband?

    B: I call _____ during lunch.

5.  A: When do you visit your parents?

    B: I visit _____ on weekends.

6.  A: When do you check your email messages?

    B: I check _____ when I wake up.

7.  A: When do you listen to the radio?

    B: I listen to _____ in the car.

8.  A: When do you talk to your teacher, Mrs. Davis?

    B: I talk to _____ after class.

9:  A: When do you see Mr. Gomez?

    B: I see _____ in class.

▶ **Practice 17. Object pronouns.** (Chart 6-4)
Choose the correct response for each question.

1.  Where do you buy organic apples?
    a. I buy at the farmers' market.    (b.) I buy them at the farmers' market.

2.  When do you see the manager, Mr. Owens?
    a. I see him on Mondays.         b. I see on Mondays.

3.  When do you get your newspaper?
    a. I get in the morning.         b. I get it in the morning.

4.  Where do you watch TV?
    a. I watch in the living room.   b. I watch it in the living room.

5.  What time do you set your alarm clock for?
    a. I set it for 7:00 A.M.        b. I set for 7:00 A.M.

▶ **Practice 18. Subject and object pronouns.** (Chart 6-4)
Use pronouns to complete the sentences.

1.  A: How are Mr. and Mrs. Carson?

    B: _____*They*_____ are fine. _____*They*_____ are taking care of their

       grandchildren right now.  They enjoy taking care of _____*them*_____.

2. A: Do you know Nathan and Vince?

   B: Yes, I do. _____ are in my chemistry class. I sit behind
   _____. _____ help me with my homework. The class is
   really hard, and I don't always understand _____.

3. A: That's Ms. Williams. Do you know _____?

   B: Yes, I do. _____ is the kindergarten teacher. The kids love
   _____.

4. A: Would you like to join Paul and me for dinner this evening?

   B: Yes, _____ would. Thank you. Can I bring something? Do you want
   _____ to bring a salad?

   A: No, thanks. Paul is cooking, and _____ has everything he needs.

▶ **Practice 19. Review: subject and object pronouns and possessive adjectives.**
   (Charts 2-5 and 6-4)
   Review the information. Complete the sentences.

| SUBJECT PRONOUNS | POSSESSIVE ADJECTIVES | OBJECT PRONOUNS |
|---|---|---|
| I | my | me |
| you | your | you |
| she | her | her |
| he | his | him |
| it | its | it |
| we | our | us |
| they | their | them |

1. I have a book. _____My_____ book is red. Please give it to _____me_____.

2. You have a book. _____Your_____ book is red. I'm giving it to _____you_____.

3. She has a book. _____ book is red. Please give it to _____.

4. He has a book. _____ book is red. Please give it to _____.

5. We have books. _____ books are red. Please give them to _____.

6. They have books. _____ books are red. Please give them to _____.

7. I have a female cat. _____ fur is black. I like to play with _____.

8. I have a male cat. _____ fur is brown. I like to play with _____.

9. My new car is blue. _____ seats are red. I love driving _____.

▶ **Practice 20. Review: subject and object pronouns and possessive adjectives.**
(Charts 2-5 and 6-4)
Complete each sentence with the correct word.

1. Hi. (*I / My / Me*) _____My_____ name is Kathy. How are you?

2. This isn't my textbook. It doesn't belong to (*I / my / me*) _____.

3. Where is Jon? I don't see (*he / his / him*) _____. I don't see
   (*he / his / him*) _____ bike.

4. Your dress is beautiful. Is (*it / your / she*) _____ new?

5. Do (*you / your / you're*) _____ have a map? We are lost.

6. We have two young children. (*We / Our / Us*) _____ son is three, and
   (*we / our / us*) _____ daughter is five.

7. Dogs like to hide (*it / their / them*) _____ bones.

▶ **Practice 21. Review: subject and object pronouns and possessive adjectives.**
(Charts 2-5 and 6-4)
Complete each sentence with the correct word.

1. Frederick is an artist. (*He / His / Him*) _____He_____
   draws cartoons. (*He / His / Him*) _____
   cartoons are very funny. I like to watch (*he / his / him*)
   _____ when he draws.

2. The kids are doing (*they / them / their*) _____
   homework. (*They / Them / Their*) _____ are working hard.
   Sometimes I help (*they / them / their*) _____ with (*they / them / their*)
   _____ homework.

3. Mary is a surgeon. (*She / Her*) _____ works long hours. (*She / Her*)
   _____ family doesn't see (*she / her*) _____ very
   much.

4. Mr. and Mrs. Cook are on vacation. I am taking care of (*they / them / their*)
   _____ dog and cat. (*They / Them / Their*) _____ dog
   likes to play, but (*they / them / their*) _____ cat likes to sleep.

5. My husband and (*I / me / my*) _____ own a restaurant together.
   We enjoy (*we / our / us*) _____ work. Sometimes (*we / our / us*)
   _____ friends and family help (*we / our / us*) _____
   at the restaurant.

▶ **Practice 22. Singular and plural nouns.** (Chart 6-5)
Complete the lists with the correct forms of the given nouns.

| **Singular** | **Plural** |
|---|---|
| 1. _____box_____ | boxes |
| 2. tomato | _____ |
| 3. zoo | _____ |
| 4. _____ | pens |
| 5. baby | _____ |
| 6. key | _____ |
| 7. _____ | cities |
| 8. _____ | wives |
| 9. dish | _____ |
| 10. thief | _____ |

▶ **Practice 23. Singular and plural nouns.** (Chart 6-5)
Write the plural form of the noun in the correct column.

| baby | city | girl | lady | life | potato | tax | tray |
|---|---|---|---|---|---|---|---|
| bush | ✓ coin | glass | ✓ leaf | party | shoe | thief | wife |

| **-s** | **-ies** | **-ves** | **-es** |
|---|---|---|---|
| _____coins_____ | _____ | _____leaves_____ | _____ |
| _____ | _____ | _____ | _____ |
| _____ | _____ | _____ | _____ |
| _____ | _____ | _____ | _____ |

▶ **Practice 24. Spelling of nouns.** (Chart 6-5)
Complete each sentence with the plural form of the noun in parentheses.

1. (*Potato*) _____Potatoes_____ are my favorite vegetable.

2. Where are the car (*key*) _____?

3. The English (*class*) _____ meet in the afternoon.

4. The police want to catch the car (*thief*) _____ soon.

5. The students are studying for their (*test*) _____.

6. (*Baby*) _____ don't like loud noises.

7. I need two (box) _____ for these gifts.

8. Why does Richard have three (radio) _____ in his kitchen?

9. During the holidays, we go to many (party) _____.

10. Miriam has ten (cat) _____ in her apartment.

11. The (match) _____ are wet.  They don't work.

12. How many (textbook) _____ do you need for your English class?

13. I like (dictionary) _____ with easy definitions.

14. Do you think cats have nine (life) _____?

15. Before you cook carrots, you need to cut off the (top)
    _____.

16. The wind is blowing the (leaf)
    _____ off the trees.

carrots

17. They make good (sandwich) _____ at that restaurant.

▶ **Practice 25. Irregular plural nouns.** (Chart 6-6)
Complete each sentence with the plural form of the appropriate noun.

| child | foot | mouse | ✓ tooth |
| fish | man | sheep | woman |

1. A dentist fixes _____ teeth _____.

2. Cats like to catch _____.

3. Are men and _____ very different?

4. There are many different kinds of _____ in the sea.

5. We put shoes on our _____.

6. In your culture, do _____ and women have the same freedoms?

7. Some movies are very violent.  They are not good for _____.

8. Baby lambs become _____.

a lamb

► **Practice 26. Complete/incomplete sentences.** (Charts 6-1 → 6-6)
Check (✓) the incorrect sentences and correct them. <u>Remember:</u> A *complete sentence* is a group of words that has a subject and a verb. An *incomplete sentence* is a group of words that does not have a subject and a verb.

          *work*
1.  ✓   I ∧ in my home office in the morning.
2. ____ My parents work at a university.
3. ____ My father in the library.
4. ____ Is a teacher.
5. ____ My mother a professor.
6. ____ Is an excellent professor.
7. ____ I study at the university.
8. ____ The university many interesting and useful classes.
9. ____ Education is important for my family.

► **Practice 27. Review.** (Charts 6-1 → 6-6)
Choose the correct completion for each sentence.

1. Where do ____ live?
   a. she        b. he        ⓒ you        d. them

2. Dr. Ruiz is my dentist and neighbor. ____ is very helpful.
   a. We        b. She        c. They        d. You

3. This is our apartment. ____ is very comfortable.
   a. It        b. We        c. She        d. He

4. These are our seats. Do you want to sit next to ____?
   a. we        b. our        c. it        d. us

5. The students are going to the movies. Their teacher is taking ____.
   a. we        b. us        c. they        d. them

6. Many ____ in the neighborhood work from their homes.
   a. womens        b. woman        c. women        d. womans

7. You and ____ like to read the same books and listen to the same music.
   a. me        b. I        c. him        d. her

8. Paul is an active child. Children like to play with ____.
   a. her        b. he        c. him        d. she

9. ____ bird has a vocabulary of fifteen words.
   a. Our        b. We        c. I        d. Us

10. I love ____.
   a. China food        b. food Chinese        c. food China        d. Chinese food

► **Practice 28. Possessive pronouns and possessive adjectives.** (Chart 6-7)
Complete each sentence with the correct possessive pronoun (*mine, yours*, etc.) or possessive adjective (*my, your*, etc.).

1. It's his car. It's _____ *his* _____.

2. It's her car. It's _____.

3. They're our cars. They're _____.

4. It's my car. It's _____.

5. It's your car. It's _____.

6. It's their car. It's _____.

7. The car belongs to her. It's _____ *her* _____ car.

8. The car belongs to me. It's _____ car.

9. The car belongs to him. It's _____ car.

10. The car belongs to them. It's _____ car.

11. The car belongs to you. It's _____ car.

12. The car belongs to us. It's _____ car.

► **Practice 29. Possessive nouns.** (Chart 6-8)
Choose the meaning of each noun in **bold**: "one" or "more than one."

|  |  | **How Many?** |  |
|---|---|---|---|
| 1. My **friends'** parents are very friendly. | one | ⟨more than one⟩ |
| 2. The **dog's** toys are all over the yard. | one | more than one |

| 3. Where is your **parents'** house? | one | more than one |
|---|---|---|
| 4. The **doctors'** offices are near the hospital. | one | more than one |
| 5. The **doctor's** offices are near the hospital. | one | more than one |
| 6. Our **co-worker's** schedule changes every week. | one | more than one |
| 7. Your **daughters'** bedroom is very large. | one | more than one |

► **Practice 30. Possessive nouns.** (Chart 6-8)
Complete each sentence with the correct nouns.

1. Jim's dog is active.

   The _____*dog*_____ belongs to _____*Jim*_____.

2. Bill's car is new.

   The _____ belongs to _____.

3. The teacher's desk is next to mine.

   The _____ belongs to _____.

4. The students' schedules are ready.

   The _____ belong to _____.

5. I'm going to buy my parents' truck.

   The _____ belongs to _____.

6. Where are the professors' offices?

   The _____ belong to _____.

► **Practice 31. Possessive nouns** (Chart 6-8)
Add an apostrophe (') where necessary.

1. Where is Ben's calculator?
2. Dans daughter is a university professor.
3. Who has the teachers pen?
4. My sisters baby doesn't sleep very much.
5. Dr. Smiths nurse is very helpful.
6. My pets names are Ping and Pong.
7. All our neighbors yards have flower and vegetable gardens.
8. What is your mothers maiden* name?

**APPLICATION FORM**

| Name: | *Sanchez,* | *Rosa* | *T* |
|---|---|---|---|
| | (last) | (first) | (middle initial) |

Address: *720 Lake Street, Green Hills, Texas*

Phone number: *253 — 555 — 7063*

Mother's maiden name: *Santos*

*Maiden name* is a married woman's last name (family name) before she got married.

► **Practice 32. Possessive nouns.** (Chart 6-8)
Add **'s** where necessary or **Ø** (nothing).

1. Tom _'s_____ job is very interesting.

2. Tom ___Ø____ works for a large airline.

3. Tom _____ buys airplanes.

4. Tom _____ wife, Olga, works at home.

5. Olga _____ designs web pages.

6. Olga _____ is artistic.

7. Olga _____ websites are very creative.

► **Practice 33. Possessive nouns.** (Chart 6-8)
Read the story. Then complete each sentence with the correct possessive name.

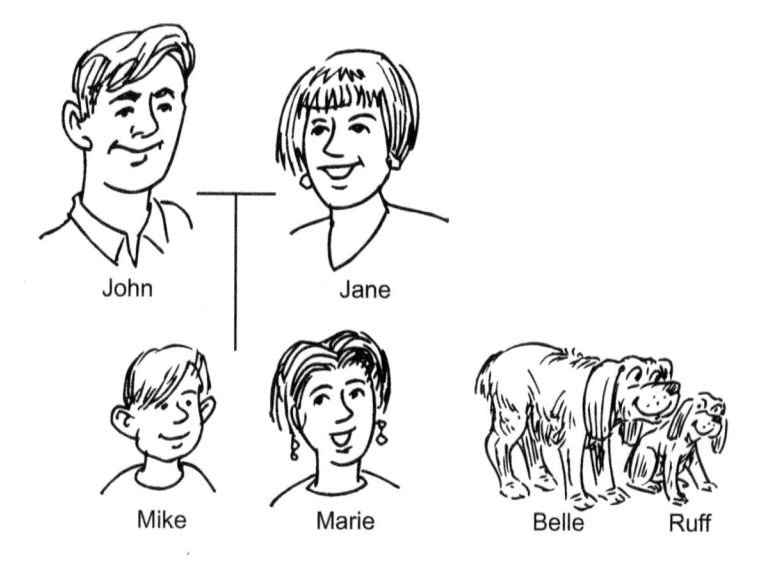

John     Jane

Mike     Marie     Belle   Ruff

Jane and John are married. They have one son and one daughter. Their son is Mike and their daughter is Marie. They also have two dogs: Belle and her puppy, Ruff.

1. Jane is _____John's_____ wife.

2. John is _____ husband.

3. Marie is _____ sister.

4. Belle is _____ mother.

5. Mike is _____ brother.

6. Ruff is _____ son.

7. Mike is Jane and _____ son.

8. Marie is John and _____ daughter.

► **Practice 34. Possessive noun or *is*.** (Chart 6-8)
Circle the meaning of *'s*: possessive or *is*.

| | | | |
|---|---|---|---|
| 1. | Bob's happy. | possessive | (is) |
| 2. | Bob's bird sounds happy. | possessive | is |
| 3. | My teacher's not at school today. | possessive | is |
| 4. | The substitute teacher's nice. | possessive | is |
| 5. | Bill's manager went on vacation. | possessive | is |
| 6. | Bill's managing the office. | possessive | is |
| 7. | Bill's a good manager. | possessive | is |
| 8. | Bill's co-workers like him. | possessive | is |

► **Practice 35. *Whose* and *who's*.** (Chart 6-9)
Choose the correct response for each sentence.

1. Whose are these?
   (a.) Pat's.                    b. Pat.

2. Who's on the phone?
   a. Mr. Smith.                  b. Mr. Smith's.

3. Who's coming?
   a. Some teachers.              b. Some teachers'.

4. Whose sweater is on the chair?
   a. Pam.                        b. Pam's.

5. Who's going to help you with your homework?
   a. Andy.                       b. Andy's.

6. Whose schedule do you have?
   a. Mark.                       b. Mark's.

7. Whose is this?
   a. My.                         b. Mine.

► **Practice 36. *Whose*.** (Chart 6-9)
Make questions with ***Whose***.

1. book \ this _____*Whose book is this?*_____

2. glasses \ these _____

3. toy \ this _____

4. keys \ these _____

5. shoes \ these _____

6. shirt \ this _____

7. cell phone \ this _____

8. pens \ these _____

▶ **Practice 37. Whose and who's.** (Chart 6-9)
Complete the sentences with **Whose** or **Who's**.

1. _____Who's_____ that?

2. _____ is that?

3. _____ coming?

4. _____ ready?

5. _____ glasses are these?

6. _____ lunch is this?

7. _____ car is in the driveway?

8. _____ working tomorrow?

9. _____ outside?

10. _____ work is this?

▶ **Practice 38. Whose.** (Chart 6-9)
Make questions with the given words.

1. is \ project \ that \ whose

_____Whose project is that?_____

2. whose \ are \ children \ those

_____

3. who \ next \ is

_____

4. are \ whose \ shoes \ in the middle of the floor

_____

5. today \ absent \ is \ who

_____

6. package \ whose \ this \ is

_____

► **Practice 39. Regular and irregular possessives.** (Charts 6-8 and 6-10)
Circle the meaning of each noun in **bold**: "one" or "more than one."

**How many?**

1. The **dogs'** food is in the kitchen.                        one     (more than one)
2. The **cat's** dishes are in the garage.                       one     more than one
3. The **teachers'** office is near the classrooms.              one     more than one
4. That **woman's** grandkids are noisy.                          one     more than one
5. Where is the **women's** clothing department?                 one     more than one
6. Is there a **men's** restroom nearby?                          one     more than one
7. The **man's** children are waiting outside.                   one     more than one
8. The **child's** toys are on the floor.                         one     more than one
9. The **children's** toys aren't in the closet.                 one     more than one

► **Practice 40. Regular and irregular possessives.** (Charts 6-8 and 6-10)
Make possessive phrases with the given words.

1. (one)    *boy \ truck*            the _____ *boy's truck* _____
2. (five)   *boys \ trucks*          the _____ *boys' trucks* _____
3. (three)  *girls \ bikes*          the _____
4. (one)    *girl \ bike*            the _____
5. (four)   *children \ toys*        the _____
6. (six)    *students \ passwords*   the _____
7. (one)    *woman \ wages*          the _____
8. (five)   *women \ wages*          the _____
9. (two)    *people \ ideas*         some _____
10. (one)   *person \ ideas*         a _____
11. (two)   *men \ coats*            the _____

▶ **Practice 41. Regular and irregular possessives.** (Charts 6-8 and 6-10)
Check (✓) the incorrect sentences and correct them.

                *children's*
1. ✓ The ~~childrens'~~ school is down the street.
2. ____ Several student's parents help at school.
3. ____ I have one brother. I like my brother's friends'.
4. ____ My brother's friend is very funny.
5. ____ I offered to fix my neighbor's computer.
6. ____ I like hearing other peoples' opinions.
7. ____ Womans' opinions are frequently different from men's opinions.
8. ____ Do you and your husband's agree very often?

▶ **Practice 42. Review.** (Charts 6-7 → 6-10)
Choose the correct completions.

1. This newspaper is yours. That newspaper is ____.
   a. our        (b.) ours        c. our's        d. ours'

2. My ____ name is Ernesto.
   a. father        b. fathers        c. fathers'        d. father's

3. ____ books are these?
   a. Who's        b. Whose        c. Who        d. Who are

4. ____ coming to the party?
   a. Who's        b. Whose        c. Who        d. Who are

5. I found two ____ backpacks in the park.
   a. girls        b. girl's        c. girls'        d. girl

6. My ____ are older than me.
   a. brother        b. brother's        c. brothers        d. brothers'

7. My ____ teacher is very patient.
   a. children's        b. childrens'        c. childs'        d. children

8. This is our hotel room and that room is ____.
   a. theirs'        b. their's        c. their        d. theirs

# Chapter 7
## Count and Noncount Nouns

▶ **Practice 1. Singular and plural.** (Chart 7-1)
Write "S" for singular or "P" for plural in front of each noun.

1. ___S___ boy
2. _____ boys
3. _____ car
4. _____ job

5. _____ passengers
6. _____ house
7. _____ apartments
8. _____ computer

▶ **Practice 2. Singular and plural.** (Chart 7-1)
Circle all the words that can come in front of each noun.

1. a    an    one    (five)    (a lot of)    cell phones
2. a    an    one    five    a lot of    cell phone
3. a    an    one    five    a lot of    buses
4. a    an    one    five    a lot of    oranges
5. a    an    one    five    a lot of    mistake
6. a    an    one    five    a lot of    rules
7. a    an    one    five    a lot of    envelope

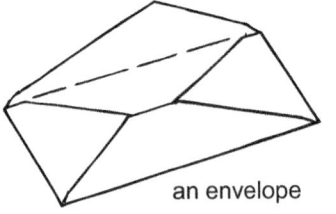

an envelope

▶ **Practice 3. Count and noncount nouns.** (Chart 7-1)
Write "C" for count or "NC" for noncount in front of each noun.

1. ___C___ girls
2. _____ girl
3. _____ homework
4. _____ traffic

5. _____ infants
6. _____ rice
7. _____ money
8. _____ coin

► **Practice 4. Count and noncount nouns.** (Chart 7-1)
Write all the correct words from the box in front of each noun.

| a | a lot of | ten |
|---|---|---|
| an | one | twenty |

1. _____ a, one _____ coin        5. _____ eggs

2. _____ coins       6. _____ ring

3. _____ water       7. _____ rings

4. _____ jewelry     8. _____ advice

► **Practice 5. Count and noncount nouns.** (Chart 7-1)
Complete each word with **-s** or **Ø** (nothing).

1. a book ___Ø___, one book _____, two book _____, fifty book _____

2. a job _____, one job _____, five job _____, a lot of job _____

3. information _____, some information _____, a lot of information _____

4. a fact _____, one fact _____, three fact _____, a lot of fact _____

► **Practice 6. Count and noncount nouns.** (Chart 7-1)
Circle all the words that can come before each noun.

1.  a     an     one     (a lot of)      homework
2.  a     an     one     a lot of        letter
3.  a     an     one     a lot of        letters
4.  a     an     one     a lot of        textbook
5.  a     an     one     a lot of        apple
6.  a     an     one     a lot of        music
7.  a     an     one     a lot of        vocabulary
8.  a     an     one     a lot of        word
9.  a     an     one     a lot of        words
10. a     an     one     a lot of        ideas

► **Practice 7. Count and noncount nouns.** (Chart 7-1)
Write a noncount noun that is close in meaning to the count noun.

|  | **Count** | **Noncount** |
|---|---|---|
| 1. | a job | _____ work _____ |
| 2. | an assignment (for school) | _____ |
| 3. | a song | _____ |

4. a word _____

5. a fact _____

6. a suggestion _____

7. a chair, a desk, a table _____

8. a banana, an apple _____

9. a coin _____

10. a ring, a bracelet _____

a bracelet

▶ **Practice 8. Noun review.** (Charts 6-4, 6-5, and 7-1)
Complete each sentence with a word from the box. Make the word plural when necessary. Use each word only one time.

| | | | |
|---|---|---|---|
| advice | fruit | ✓ money | weather |
| child | furniture | monkey | work |
| city | help | potato | |
| country | horse | tool | |
| foot | man | traffic | |

1. I have a lot of _____money_____ in my wallet. I'm rich.

2. Cowboys ride _____.

3. I would like to visit many _____ in Canada. I'd like to visit Vancouver, Victoria, Quebec City, Toronto, and some others.

4. There are three _____ in North America: Canada, the United States, and Mexico.

5. Birds and _____ live in trees.

6. Barbara has four suitcases. She can't carry all of them. She needs some _____.

7. There is a lot of _____ on the street during rush hour.

8. Susie and Bobby are seven years old. They aren't adults. They're

_____.

9. We need a new bed, a new couch, and some new chairs. We need some new

_____.

10. People wear shoes on their _____.

11. I like pears, oranges, and bananas. I eat a lot of _____.

a pear

12. Sometimes I have a steak, a salad, and French-fried _____ for dinner.

13. When the temperature is around 35°C (77°F), I'm comfortable. But I don't like very hot

_____ .

14. I'm not busy today. I don't have much

_____ to do.

a hammer

15. I have a problem. I need your help. I need some

_____ from you.

TOOLS

a saw

16. Some _____ have mustaches.

17. Where is my hammer? Do you have a saw? I need some

_____ .

a screwdriver

▶ **Practice 9. A vs. an** (Chart 7-2)
Write **a** or **an**.

1. ___an___ idea

2. _____ office

3. _____ elephant

4. _____ university

5. _____ uncle

6. _____ interesting idea

7. _____ hour

8. _____ house

9. _____ hungry animal

10. _____ upset child

▶ **Practice 10. A vs. an** (Chart 7-2)
Write **a**, **an**, or **Ø**.

1. ___Ø___ happy

2. ___a___ happy man

3. _____ exciting

4. _____ exciting day

5. _____ hot oven

6. _____ easy test

7. _____ honest man

8. _____ honest

9. _____ my father

10. _____ his job

an oven

► **Practice 11. A vs. an** (Chart 7-2)
Write **a**, **an**, or Ø.

1. I need to see ____*a*____ doctor.

2. I have _____ headache.

3. It is _____ painful.

4. Mary is reading _____ article in the newspaper.

5. The article is _____ interesting.

6. _____ healthy person gets regular exercise.

7. The Browns own _____ house.

8. Gary and Joel are having _____ argument in the cafeteria.  It is _____ uncomfortable situation.

9. I feel _____ uncomfortable.

10. Are you _____ hard worker?

11. Was the test _____ hard?

12. Janet is _____ honest person.

13. The store manager is talking to _____ angry woman.

14. Bill is _____ uncle.  He has _____ niece and two nephews.

► **Practice 12. A/an and some.** (Chart 7-3)
Write each word from the box in the correct column.

| advice | earache | elevator | furniture | letter | packages | umbrella |
|--------|---------|----------|-----------|--------|----------|----------|
| ✓ dog | eggs | flower | gardens | mail | suggestion | umbrellas |

|            *a*            |            *an*            |           *some*          |
|--------------------------|----------------------------|---------------------------|
|      _____ dog _____      |      _____      |      _____      |
|      _____      |      _____      |      _____      |
|      _____      |      _____      |      _____      |
|      _____      |       [ELEVATOR]           |      _____      |
|                            |                            |      _____      |
|                            |                            |      _____      |
|                            |                            |      _____      |

► **Practice 13. A/an and some.** (Chart 7-3)
Use *a/an* or *some*. Are the nouns singular or plural?

1. Bob has _____ a _____ book on his desk.            singular    plural

2. Bob has _____ some _____ books on his desk.        singular    plural

3. I see _____ desk in this room.             singular    plural

4. I see _____ desks in this room.            singular    plural

5. I would like _____ apple.                  singular    plural

6. The kids want _____ apples too.            singular    plural

7. Is there _____ mail for me?                singular    plural

8. I need to move _____ furniture downstairs. singular    plural

9. Did you pay _____ tax?                     singular    plural

10. Did you pay _____ taxes?                  singular    plural

▶ **Practice 14. A/an and some.** (Chart 7-3)
Complete each sentence with **a/an** or **some**.

1. Here is _____*a*_____ letter for you.

2. There is _____ mail on the kitchen table.

3. _____ teachers give a lot of homework.

4. I have _____ long assignment.

5. The teacher has _____ interesting idea for today's discussion.

6. _____ ideas take several days to discuss.

7. Dr. Roberts is _____ very special teacher.

8. He gives _____ interesting lectures.

9. Are _____ students working on their projects?

10. Is _____ assistant teacher helping them?

▶ **Practice 15. Review.** (Charts 7-1 → 7-4)
Choose all the correct sentences.

1. (a.) We are learning a lot of vocabulary.
   (b.) We are learning some vocabulary.
   c. We are learning some vocabularies.

2. a. Our teacher gives a lot of homeworks.
   b. Our teacher gives a lot of homework.
   c. Our teachers gives a lot of assignment.

3. a. Let's listen to music.
   b. Let's listen to some music.
   c. Let's listen to a music.

4. a. Do you have some advice for me?
   b. Do you have an advice for me?
   c. Do you have a suggestion for me?

5. a. I have job.
   b. I have a job.
   c. I have some job.

6. a. I would like interesting job.
   b. I would like an interesting job.
   c. I would like some interesting job.

► **Practice 16. Units of measure.** (Chart 7-4)
Write the name of the item for each picture. Use the expressions in the box.

| | | | |
|---|---|---|---|
| ✓a bag of | a box of | a carton of | |
| a bar of | a bunch of | a jar of | |
| a bottle of | a can of | a tube of | |

1. _____*a bag of rice*_____

2. _____

3. _____

4. _____

5. _____

6. _____

7. _____

8. _____

9. _____

► **Practice 17. Units of measure.** (Chart 7-4)
What can you find at a store or restaurant? Complete each phrase with nouns from the box.
You may use some nouns more than once.

| | | | | |
|---|---|---|---|---|
| bananas | ✓ cereal | ice cream | mayonnaise | ✓ rice |
| bread | cheese | lettuce | paper | water |

1. a box of _____*cereal, rice, paper*_____

2. a sheet of _____

3. a head of _____

4. a piece of _____

5. a loaf of _____

6. a bunch of _____

7. a bowl of _____

8. a bottle of _____

9. a jar of _____

▶ **Practice 18. Review: *A/an/some* and units of measure.** (Charts 7-3 and 7-4)
Complete the sentences with *a*, *an*, or *some*.

1. I'm hungry. I'd like . . .

   a. _____*a*_____ piece of chicken.

   b. _____ fruit

   c. _____ food

   d. _____ bowl of ice cream

   e. _____ apple

   f. _____ can of soup

   g. _____ rice

   h. _____ strawberries

   strawberries

2. I'm thirsty. I'd like . . .

   a. _____*some*_____ water

   b. _____ bottle of water

   c. _____ juice

   d. _____ glass of milk

   e. _____ cup of coffee

   f. _____ strong coffee

   g. _____ tea

   h. _____ milk

▶ **Practice 19. Much/many.** (Chart 7-5)
Complete the sentences with **much** or **many**.

I need to go to the store. I don't have . . .

1. _____*much*_____ coffee
2. _____ bananas
3. _____ fruit
4. _____ lamb
5. _____ rice

6. _____ sugar
7. _____ bread
8. _____ food
9. _____ peaches
10. _____ cans of soup

peaches

▶ **Practice 20. A few/a little.** (Chart 7-5)
Complete the sentences with **a few** or **a little**.

I need to go shopping. I need . . .

1. _____*a little*_____ salt
2. _____ strawberries
3. _____ pens
4. _____ cheese
5. _____ tea
6. _____ teabags

7. _____ bottles of water
8. _____ sandwiches
9. _____ flour
10. _____ rolls of toilet paper

a teabag

▶ **Practice 21. Much/many/a few/a little.** (Chart 7-5)
Choose the correct words. Add **-s** or **Ø** (nothing) to the nouns where necessary.

1. The teacher needs (*a few* / ⟨*a little*⟩) information __Ø__ about her students.

2. Do the students have (*much* / ⟨*many*⟩) question _s____?

3. Here are (*a few* / *a little*) new pen _____ for you.

4. Do you have (*a few* / *a little*) minute _____ to talk?

5. Andy doesn't drink (*much / many*) coffee _____. He drinks (*a few / a little*) tea _____.

6. There are (*much / many*) beautiful flowers _____ in your garden.

7. I have (*a few / a little*) flower _____ in my garden and (*much / many*) vegetable _____.

▶ **Practice 22. How much/how many.** (Chart 7-5)
Rick is going shopping. His roommate gives him a list. He needs to know the amount to buy.
Write questions with **How much/How many . . . do we need?**

| ✓ carrots | eggs | fruit |
| cheese | flour | olive oil |

1. _____ *How many carrots do we need?* _____

2. _____

3. _____

4. _____

5. _____

6. _____

▶ **Practice 23. First mention vs. second mention.** (Chart 7-6)
Complete each sentence with *the* or *a*.

1. These pants and shirts don't fit. ___*The*___ pants are too big, and _____ shirts are too tight.

2. Here's some chicken. Be careful! _____ chicken is very spicy.

3. Andrew drives _____ company truck. _____ truck is big and uses a lot of gas. His company pays for _____ gas.

4. Rudy wants to give his wife _____ ring for their anniversary. _____ ring has three diamonds, and _____ diamonds are very large.

5. Rachel is looking at _____ picture of _____ dog and _____ baby. _____ baby is sleeping, and _____ dog is watching her.

6. Tommy is getting _____ new bike for his birthday. _____ bike is very fast, and he is excited to ride it.

7. Dr. Olsson is speaking with _____ new patient. _____ patient is scared because she needs emergency surgery.

8. Do you have _____ minute? I have _____ problem and would like your advice.

▶ **Practice 24. General vs. specific.** (Chart 7-7)
Decide if the word in *italics* has a general or specific meaning.

1. *Clothes* are expensive.            (general)    specific

2. The *clothes* in Jan's closet are expensive.    general    specific

3. *Lemons* are sour.           general    specific

4. I love *vegetables*.          general    specific

5. The *vegetables* on the counter are from my garden.    general    specific

6. How are the *carrots* in your salad?  Are they sweet?    general    specific

7. *Rabbits* like carrots.         general    specific

8. What are you doing about the *rabbits* in your garden?    general    specific

▶ **Practice 25. General vs. specific.** (Chart 7-7)
Complete the sentences with **a/an**, **the**, or **Ø** (nothing).

1. I need ____Ø____ sugar for my coffee.

2. _____ sugar is in the cupboard.

3. Dentists say _____ sugar is not good for our teeth.

4. I'd like _____ glass of water.

5. Ann would like _____ orange for a snack.

6. _____ oranges grow on trees.

7. Ken has _____ egg every day for lunch.

8. Are _____ eggs healthy?

9. I'm going shopping.  I need _____ bread and _____ cheese.

10. Jack is having _____ rice, _____ fish, and _____ bowl of soup for dinner.

11. Johnny, please feed _____ cat.  He's hungry.

12. Do you like _____ cats? Would you like _____ cat?

## ▶ Practice 26. Article review. (Charts 7-3, 7-6, and 7-7)
Choose the sentence that is closest in meaning to the given situation.

1. Mark is at a toy store. There are five fire trucks. He buys one for his son.
   a. He buys a fire truck.        b. He buys the fire truck.

2. Pat is at a pet store. There is one turtle. She buys it.
   a. She buys a turtle.           b. She buys the turtle.

3. Martha is leaving her apartment. There are three bags near the door. She takes one.
   a. She takes the bag.           b. She takes a bag.

4. Jane is sitting outside in her garden. It is midnight. She is looking up at the sky.
   a. She sees the moon.           b. She sees a moon.

5. I love ice cream. Vanilla ice cream is my favorite.
   a. I love the vanilla ice cream.     b. I love vanilla ice cream.

6. Alice is picking apples from an apple tree. It has only five apples. She picks all five.
   a. She takes the apples home.        b. She takes apples home.

7. Paul drives a small car. He wants to save gas.
   a. He doesn't like to drive big cars.     b. He doesn't like to drive the big cars.

## ▶ Practice 27. Some/any. (Chart 7-8)
Choose the correct word. In some cases, both words are correct.

1. Let's go outside. I need (*some* / *any*) fresh air.

2. There aren't (*some* / *any*) clouds in the sky.

3. There is (*some* / *any*) wind.

4. I don't feel (*some* / *any*) wind.

5. Do you have (*some* / *any*) time?

6. Sorry, I don't have (*some* / *any*) time right now.

7. I have (*some* / *any*) time tomorrow.

8. I need (*some* / *any*) money for the store.

9. Do you have (*some* / *any*) money?

10. (*Some* / *Any*) people carry a lot of money in their wallets.

▶ **Practice 28. Some/any.** (Charts 7-3 and 7-8)

Think about shopping. Write sentences about what you need and don't need. Use *some/any* and the words from the list. Add *-s/-es* where necessary. You can also use your own words.

| | | | | |
|---|---|---|---|---|
| avocado | egg | fruit | potato | soup |
| banana | fish | grape | rice | toothpaste |
| coffee | flour | meat | soap | vegetable |

1. I need _____, _____, _____,

_____, and _____.

2. I don't need _____, _____,

_____, _____, or _____.

an avocado          grapes

▶ **Practice 29. A/an or any.** (Chart 7-8)

Circle *a*, *an*, or *any*. Remember, use *any* with noncount nouns and plural count nouns. Use *a* with singular count nouns.

I don't want . . .

1. (a)      an      any      low grade on my test.

2. a      an      any      low grades this year.

3. a      an      any      pets.

4. a      an      any      pet.

5. a      an      any      ice cream for dessert.

6. a      an      any      bowl of ice cream for dessert.

7. a      an      any      cup of coffee.

8. a      an      any      help.

9. a      an      any      homework.

10. a      an      any      assignment.

11. a      an      any      assignments.

▶ **Practice 30. A/any.** (Chart 7-8)

Use *any* or *a*. Use *any* with noncount nouns and plural count nouns. Use *a* with singular count nouns.

1. I don't have _____*any*_____ money.

2. I don't have _____*a*_____ job.

3. I don't have _____*any*_____ brothers or sisters.

4. We don't need to buy _____ new furniture.

5. Mr. and Mrs. Kelly don't have _____ children.

6. There isn't _____ coffee in the house.

7. Ann doesn't want _____ cup of coffee.

8. I don't like this room because there aren't _____ windows.

9. Amanda is very unhappy because she doesn't have _____ friends.

10. I don't need _____ help. I can finish my homework by myself.

11. I don't have _____ comfortable chair in my dorm room.

12. I'm getting along fine. I don't have _____ problems.

13. Joe doesn't have _____ car, so he takes the bus to school.

14. I don't have _____ homework to do tonight.

15. I don't need _____ new clothes.

16. I don't need _____ new suit.

▶ **Practice 31. Review.** (Chapter 7)

Draw a line through the expressions that <u>cannot</u> complete the sentences.

1. I need to buy ____ white sugar.

   a. a
   b. an
   c. some
   d. any
   e. two
   f. a lot of
   g. a bag of
   h. Ø

2. I don't need ____ brown sugar.

   a. some
   b. much
   c. a
   d. a lot of
   e. any
   f. two
   g. three bags of
   h. Ø

3. Do you need _____ flour?

    a. an

    b. any

    c. a

    d. a bag of

    e. some

    f. two bags of

    g. a lot of

    h. Ø

▶ **Practice 32. Review.** (Chapter 7)
Correct the mistakes.

*countries*
1. Korea and Japan are ~~country~~ in Asia.
2. Is there many traffics at 5:00 P.M.?
3. Are you a hungry? Do you want some food?
4. My children come home every day with a lot of homeworks.
5. The digital cameras take wonderful pictures.
6. My eggs and coffee don't taste very good. Eggs are very salty, and coffee is weak.
7. What do you like better for a snack: orange or the orange juice?
8. I wear dresses for work and the jeans at home.
9. I'm going to bank. I need money.
10. We need to get any furniture. Do you know good furniture store?

# Chapter 8
# Expressing Past Time, Part 1

▶ **Practice 1. Simple past forms of be.** (Chart 8-1)
Complete the sentences with the correct form of **be**.

|  | **Now** | **An hour ago** |
|---|---|---|
| 1. | I am tired. | I _____was_____ tired. |
| 2. | We are tired. | We _____ tired. |
| 3. | She is tired. | She _____ tired. |
| 4. | They are tired. | They _____ tired. |
| 5. | He is tired. | He _____ tired. |
| 6. | The cat is tired. | The cat _____ tired. |
| 7. | My kids are tired. | My kids _____ tired. |
| 8. | Al and Todd are tired. | Al and Todd _____ tired. |
| 9. | Our teacher is tired. | Our teacher _____ tired. |
| 10. | You are tired. | You _____ tired. |

▶ **Practice 2. Past forms of be.** (Chart 8-1)
Choose the correct form of the verb in each sentence.

1. My parents (*was* / (*were*)) at home last night.
2. Our next-door neighbors (*was* / *were*) at work.
3. I (*was* / *were*) at the library.
4. My roommate (*was* / *were*) there too.
5. She (*was* / *were*) across the table from me.
6. Our teacher (*was* / *were*) at the table next to us.
7. He (*was* / *were*) half-asleep.
8. We (*was* / *were*) at the library until closing time.
9. The library (*was* / *were*) open until 9:00 P.M.
10. My roommate and I (*was* / *were*) the last people to leave.

► **Practice 3. Past forms of be: negative.** (Chart 8-2)
Complete the sentences with the correct negative form: ***wasn't*** or ***weren't***.

1. I _____ *wasn't* _____ at school yesterday.

2. You _____ at school yesterday.

3. Some students _____ at school yesterday.

4. They _____ at school yesterday.

5. Toshi _____ at school yesterday.

6. He _____ at school yesterday.

7. My teacher _____ at school yesterday.

8. Beth and Mark _____ at school yesterday.

9. Sarah _____ at school yesterday.

10. She and I _____ at school yesterday.

11. We _____ at school yesterday.

► **Practice 4. Simple past tense of be: negative.** (Chart 8-2)
Complete the sentences with the correct negative form: ***wasn't*** or ***weren't***.

A bad hotel

1. The hotel _____ *wasn't* _____ nice.

2. My room _____ clean.

3. The beds _____ comfortable.

4. The pillows _____ soft.

5. The shower water _____ warm.

6. The elevators _____ fast.

7. The restaurant _____ good.

8. The food _____ fresh.

9. The hotel clerks _____ polite.

► **Practice 5. Simple past tense of *be*: negative.** (Chart 8-2)
Write sentences about the people in the chart.

|  | **Mike** | **Lori** | **Ricardo** | **Eva** |
|---|---|---|---|---|
| at work | x |  |  |  |
| at school |  |  |  |  |
| on vacation |  |  | x |  |
| out of town |  | x |  | x |

Where were they yesterday?

1. Mike _____wasn't out of town yesterday. He was at work._____

2. Ricardo _____

3. Lori _____

4. Lori and Eva _____

► **Practice 6. Simple past tense of *be*: negative.** (Chart 8-2)
Think about your elementary school years. Write sentences about yourself. Use *was* or
*wasn't*.

1. (*shy*) _____I was / wasn't shy._____     4. (*active*) _____

2. (*happy*) _____     5. (*serious*) _____

3. (*quiet*) _____     6. (*noisy*) _____

► **Practice 7. Simple past tense of *be*: questions.** (Chart 8-3)
Complete the questions with *Was* or *Were*.

1. _____Were_____ you home yesterday evening?

2. _____ your husband home yesterday evening?

3. _____ he home yesterday evening?

4. _____ your parents home last weekend?

5. _____ they home last weekend?

6. _____ I home last weekend?

7. _____ the teacher home last night?

8. _____ your teacher home last night?

9. _____ Jan and I home yesterday evening?

10. _____ we home last weekend?

► **Practice 8. Simple past tense of *be*: questions.** (Chart 8-3)
Make two questions for each situation. The first question is a yes/no question, and the second is a *where* question. Give the answers for both questions. Use the places from the box.

| at the grocery store | at the library | at the train station |
| at home | at the mall | at the zoo |

1. Jake and Kevin \ at a swimming pool

   A: _____Were Jake and Kevin at a swimming pool?_____

   B: _____No, they weren't._____

   A: _____Where were they?_____

   B: _____They were at the grocery store._____

2. Ellen \ at the library

   A: _____

   B: _____

   A: _____

   B: _____

3. you \ at a party

   A: _____

   B: _____

   A: _____

   B: _____

4. Thomas \ at the airport

   A: _____

   B: _____

   A: _____

   B: _____

5. your kids \ at school

   A: _____

   B: _____

   A: _____

   B: _____

6. Liz and you \ at the park

A: _____

B: _____

A: _____

B: _____

▶ **Practice 9. Simple past tense of *be*: questions.** (Chart 8-3)
Your friend was at a movie last night. Ask questions about the movie. Use *was* or *were*.

1. _____*Was*_____ it scary?

2. _____ you afraid?

3. _____ the characters interesting?

4. _____ the movie funny?

5. _____ the main actor good?

6. _____ she or he a good actor?

7. _____ the actors good?

8. _____ they good?

▶ **Practice 10. Simple past tense -*ed*.** (Chart 8-4)
Complete the sentences with the simple past tense form of the verbs.

| **Every day** | **Yesterday** |
|---|---|
| 1. I study English. | I _____*studied*_____ English. |
| 2. He studies English. | He _____ English. |
| 3. We walk in the park. | We _____ in the park. |
| 4. You work hard. | You _____ hard. |
| 5. They smile. | They _____ . |
| 6. The baby smiles. | The baby _____ |
| 7. Sonja talks on the phone. | Sonja _____ on the phone. |
| 8. Tim helps his parents. | Tim _____ his parents. |
| 9. I help my parents. | I _____ my parents. |
| 10. She listens carefully. | She _____ carefully. |
| 11. They listen carefully. | They _____ carefully. |

▶ **Practice 11. Simple past tense -ed.** (Chart 8-4)
Look at the activities and write sentences about the people.

| Yesterday | Ruth | Deb | Bill | Stuart |
|---|---|---|---|---|
| cook breakfast | x | | x | |
| watch TV | | x | x | |
| talk to friends on the phone | x | | | |
| exercise at a gym | | | | x |

1. Deb ____*watched TV.*_____

2. Stuart _____

3. Ruth and Bill _____

4. Ruth also _____

5. Bill also _____

▶ **Practice 12. Simple past tense -ed.** (Chart 8-4)
Complete each sentence with the simple past tense form of a verb from the box.

**Group A:**

| asked | erased | kissed | touched | ✓ watched |
|---|---|---|---|---|
| cooked | finished | laughed | walked | worked |
| coughed | helped | stopped | washed | |

1. I _____*watched*_____ TV last night.

2. Anna _____ to class yesterday instead of taking the bus.

3. I _____ the dirty dishes after dinner last night.

4. Jim _____ the board with an eraser.

5. Robert loves his daughter. He _____ her on the forehead.

6. The joke was funny. We _____ at the funny story.

7. The train suddenly _____.
   There was a cow on the tracks.

8. I cleaned for three hours last night. I
   _____ my housework at
   about nine o'clock.

9. Steve _____ my shoulder
   with his hand to get my attention.

10. Mr. Wilson _____ in his garden yesterday morning.

11. Judy _____ a lot. She had a bad cold.

12. Dan is a good cook. He _____ some delicious food last night.

13. Linda _____ a question in class yesterday.

14. I had a problem with my homework. The teacher _____ me
    before class.

## Group B:

| arrived | killed | remembered | smiled |
| closed | played | shaved | sneezed |
| enjoyed | rained | signed | ✓ snowed |

15. It's winter. The ground is white because it _____ *snowed* _____ yesterday.

16. Anita _____ at the airport on September 3.

17. The girls and boys _____ baseball after school yesterday.

18. When Ali got a new credit card, he _____ his name in ink on the
    back of the card.

19. Rick had a beard yesterday, but now he doesn't. He _____ it this
    morning.

20. The students' test papers were very good. The teacher, Mr. Jackson, was very pleased.
    He _____ when he returned the test papers.

21. I _____ the party last night. It was fun. I had a good time.

22. The window was open. Mr. Chan _____ it because it was cold
    outside.

23. The streets were wet this morning because it _____ last night.

24. "Achoo!" When Judy _____, Ken said, "Bless you." Oscar said, "Gesundheit!"

25. I have my books with me. I didn't forget them today. I _____ to bring them to class.

26. Mrs. Lane was upset because there was a fly in the room. The fly was buzzing all around the room. Finally, she _____ it with a rolled-up newspaper.

**Group C:**

| added | folded | needed | waited |
|-------|--------|--------|--------|
| counted | invited | visited | ✓ wanted |

27. The children _____*wanted*_____ some candy after dinner.

28. Mr. Miller _____ to stay in the hospital for several days after his operation.

29. I _____ the number of students in the room. There were twenty.

30. Mr. and Mrs. Johnson _____ us to come to their house last Sunday.

31. Last Sunday we _____ the Johnsons. We had dinner with them.

32. I _____ the letter before I put it in the envelope.

33. Kim _____ for the bus at the corner of Fifth Avenue and Main Street.

34. The boy _____ the numbers on the board in math class yesterday.

| 8-A Summary of Spelling Rules for *-ed* Verbs | | |
|---|---|---|
| | END OF VERB- → *-ED* FORM | |
| Rule 1: | CONSONANT + *-e* → ADD *-d.* | |
| | smi*le* → smi*led* | |
| | era*se* → era*sed* | |
| Rule 2: | ONE VOWEL + ONE CONSONANT → DOUBLE THE CONSONANT.* ADD *-ed.* | |
| | st*op* | st*opped* |
| | r*ub* | r*ubbed* |
| Rule 3: | TWO VOWELS + ONE CONSONANT → ADD *-ed.* DO NOT DOUBLE THE CONSONANT. | |
| | r*ain* | r*ained* |
| | n*eed* | n*eeded* |
| Rule 4: | TWO CONSONANTS → ADD *-ed.* DO NOT DOUBLE THE CONSONANT. | |
| | cou*nt* | cou*nted* |
| | he*lp* | he*lped* |
| Rule 5: | CONSONANT + *-y* → CHANGE *-y* TO *-i.* ADD *-ed.* | |
| | stu*dy* | stu*died* |
| | car*ry* | car*ried* |
| Rule 6: | VOWEL + *-y* → ADD *-ed.* DO NOT CHANGE *-y* TO *-i.* | |
| | pl*ay* | pl*ayed* |
| | enj*oy* | enj*oyed* |

*EXCEPTIONS: Do not double *x* (*fix* + *-ed* = *fixed*). Do not double *w* (*snow* + *-ed* = *snowed*).

▶ **Practice 13. Spelling rules: *-ed* verbs.** (Chart 8-A)
Study each rule and the examples. Then write the simple past tense of the given verbs.

**Rule 1.** END OF VERB: CONSONANT + *-e* → ADD *-d.*

1. like     → _____

2. close    → _____

3. shave   → _____

4. love     → _____

5. hate     → _____

6. exercise → _____

**Rule 2.** END OF VERB: ONE VOWEL + ONE CONSONANT → DOUBLE THE CONSONANT. ADD *-ed.*

7. plan     → _____

8. drop     → _____

9. clap     → _____

**Rule 3.** END OF VERB: TWO VOWELS + ONE CONSONANT → ADD *-ed*. DO NOT DOUBLE THE CONSONANT.

10. join → _____

11. shout → _____

12. wait → _____

**Rule 4.** END OF VERB: TWO CONSONANTS → ADD *-ed*. DO NOT DOUBLE THE CONSONANT.

13. point → _____

14. touch → _____

15. melt → _____

**Rule 5.** END OF VERB: CONSONANT + *-y* → CHANGE *-y* TO *-i*. ADD *-ed*.

16. marry → _____

17. try → _____

18. hurry → _____

19. reply → _____

20. dry → _____

**Rule 6.** END OF VERB: VOWEL + *-y* → ADD *-ed*. DO NOT CHANGE *-y* TO *-i*.

21. stay → _____

22. delay → _____

▶ **Practice 14. Spelling practice: *-ed*.** (Chart 8-4)
Write the *-ed* forms of these verbs.

|  |  | *-ed* |
|---|---|---|
| 1. | count | *counted* |
| 2. | rain | _____ |
| 3. | help | _____ |
| 4. | plan | _____ |
| 5. | dream | _____ |
| 6. | erase | _____ |

_____

NOTE: Spelling rules for the two-syllable verbs *visit, answer, happen, occur, listen, open,* and *enter* are in Appendix 5 at the back of this Workbook.

7.   close   _____

8.   yawn    _____

9.   study   _____

10.  worry   _____

11.  drop    _____

▶ **Practice 15. Spelling review: -ed.** (Chart 8-4)
Use the correct form of a verb in the box to complete each sentence.

| | | | |
|---|---|---|---|
| carry | fail | rub | stop |
| clap | ✓ finish | smile | taste |
| cry | learn | stay | wait |

1.  I _____*finished*_____ my homework at nine o'clock last night.

2.  We _____ some new vocabulary yesterday.

3.  I _____ the soup before dinner last night.  It was delicious.

4.  Linda _____ for the bus at the corner yesterday.

5.  The bus _____ at the corner.  It was on time.

6.  Ann _____ her suitcases to the bus station yesterday.  They weren't heavy.

7.  The baby _____ her eyes because she was sleepy.

8.  I _____ home and watched a sad show on TV last night.  I _____ at the end of the show.

9.  Mike _____ his examination last week.  He got most answers wrong.

10. Jane _____ at her kids.  She was happy to see them.

11. The audience loved the movie.  They _____ loudly at the end.

▶ **Practice 16. Yesterday, last, and ago.** (Chart 8-5)
Complete each sentence with *yesterday*, *last*, or *ago*.

My soccer team played . . .

1. _____*last*_____ night.

2. _____ afternoon.

3. _____ Wednesday.

4. _____ week.

5. _____ summer.

6. _____ month.

7. _____ evening.

8. three months _____.

9. two weeks _____.

10. one year _____.

11. _____ morning.

12. _____ weekend.

▶ **Practice 17. Yesterday, last, and ago.** (Chart 8-5)
Rewrite each *italicized* sentence using a time expression with *yesterday*, *last*, or *ago*.

1. It's 7:00. *At 6:55, Tim brushed his teeth.*

   _____*Tim brushed his teeth five minutes ago.*_____

2. It's 3:00 P.M. *The day before at 3:00, Bonnie walked to the park.*

   _____

3. This week Tom is working. *The week before, he was at home on vacation.*

   _____

4. It's 2014. *In 2010, Sam graduated from high school.*

   _____

5. It's Saturday. *The Thursday before, Jan worked 12 hours.*

   _____

6. It's March. *The January before, Thomas stayed with his parents.*

   _____

7. It's 10:00 P.M. *The night before at 10:00, we watched a DVD.*

   _____

► **Practice 18. Irregular verbs: Group 1.** (Chart 8-6)
Complete each sentence with the simple past tense form of the verb.

| **Every day** | **Yesterday** |
|---|---|
| 1. I eat vegetables. | I _____ate_____ vegetables. |
| 2. You eat vegetables. | You _____ vegetables. |
| 3. He eats vegetables. | He _____ vegetables. |
| 4. She eats vegetables. | She _____ vegetables. |
| 5. We eat vegetables. | We _____ vegetables. |
| 6. They eat vegetables. | They _____ vegetables. |
| 7. Sam and I eat vegetables. | Sam and I _____ vegetables. |
| 8. I do my homework. | I _____ my homework. |
| 9. You do your homework. | You _____ your homework. |
| 10. He does his homework. | He _____ his homework. |
| 11. We do our homework. | We _____ our homework. |
| 12. I sleep eight hours. | I _____ eight hours. |
| 13. They sleep eight hours. | They _____ eight hours. |
| 14. We sleep eight hours. | We _____ eight hours. |
| 15. She sleeps eight hours. | She _____ eight hours. |

► **Practice 19. Irregular verbs: Group 1.** (Chart 8-6)
Which sentences are true for you? Write the present form for each verb in italics.

**Present Form**

1. _____ I *got* a package in the mail yesterday.      _____get_____

2. _____ I *came* home early yesterday.      _____

3. _____ I *went* out to dinner last night.      _____

4. _____ I *had* a headache yesterday.      _____

5. _____ I *put* on sunglasses yesterday.      _____

6. _____ I *slept* for nine hours last night.      _____

7. _____ I *saw* my parents yesterday.      _____

8. _____ I *did* homework last night.      _____

9. _____ I *ate* fish for dinner.                    _____

10. _____ I *wrote* an email last night.             _____

11. _____ I *sat* in the sun yesterday.              _____

12. _____ I *stood* outside in the rain yesterday.   _____

▶ **Practice 20. Irregular verbs: Group 1.** (Chart 8-6)
Complete each sentence with the simple past tense form of a verb from the box. In some sentences, more than one verb fits. The number in parentheses tells you how many verbs you can use.

| come | eat | go | put | sit | stand |
|------|-----|-----|-----|-----|-------|
| ✓ do | get | have | see | sleep | write |

1. Last week, I _____ *did* _____ something really fun.  (1)

2. I _____ to the mountains for a camping trip.  (1)

3. At night, I _____ under the stars.  (3)

4. I _____ millions of stars in the sky.  (1)

5. I _____ three fish from the river with my fishing pole.  (1)

6. I cooked them over a fire and _____ them for dinner.  (2)

7. One day I walked in the woods for several hours.  I _____ deer and foxes with my binoculars.  (1)

8  I _____ home late Monday night.  (3)

9. I _____ an email to my parents.  (1)

10. I _____ some photos in the email.  (2)

► **Practice 21. Simple past: negative.** (Charts 1-5 and 8-7)
Choose the true completion for each sentence.

When my parents were teenagers, they . . .

|     |        |            |                    |
| --- | ------ | ---------- | ------------------ |
| 1.  | had    | didn't have | computers.        |
| 2.  | walked | didn't walk | to school.        |
| 3.  | did    | didn't do   | chores on weekends. |
| 4.  | drank  | didn't drink | sodas.           |
| 5.  | used   | didn't use  | microwave ovens.  |
| 6.  | watched | didn't watch | videos.         |
| 7.  | talked | didn't talk | on cell phones.   |

► **Practice 22. Simple past: negative.** (Charts 1-5 and 8-7)
Complete each sentence with the negative form of the verb.

1. I came home late.          I _____*didn't come*_____ home late.

2. You came home late.        You _____ home late.

3. He came home late.         He _____ home late.

4. She came home late.        She _____ home late.

5. We came home late.         We _____ home late.

6. They came home late.       They _____ home late.

7. He played soccer.          He _____ soccer.

8. They played soccer.        They _____ soccer.

9. She answered the phone.    She _____ the phone.

10. I saw a UFO.*             I _____ a UFO.

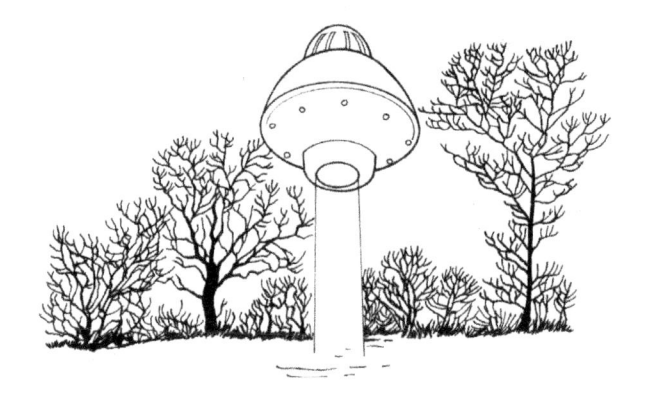

---

*UFO = unidentified flying object.

11. You slept late.                You _____ late.

12. I did my homework.          I _____ my homework.

13. I was late.                      I _____ late.

14. They were late.               They _____ late.

▶ **Practice 23. Simple past: negative.** (Chart 8-7)
Write sentences that are true for you.

1. eat \ a big dinner \ last night

   _____ *I ate a big dinner last night.* OR *I didn't eat a big dinner last night.* _____

2. sleep \ on the floor \ last night

   _____

3. write \ a long email \ earlier today

   _____

4. walk \ to school \ last month

   _____

5. get \ some money from the bank \ yesterday

   _____

6. go \ to my cousins' house\ last week

   _____

7. do \ some housework \ yesterday

   _____

8. work \ outside \ yesterday

   _____

9. put on \ my shoes \ yesterday

   _____

10. stop \ at a café \ earlier today

   _____

*Part I.* Read the story.

### A Bad Day

Derek had a lot of trouble yesterday. He woke up with a sore throat and headache. Then he dropped his breakfast of eggs on the floor. The plate broke on his foot. He cleaned up the eggs and the broken plate. Then he decided to have coffee. He found a little cream in his fridge, but when he drank the coffee, he realized the cream was sour. He decided to have breakfast at school.

Derek waited for the bus for half an hour, but it didn't come. He got his bike and went to school. During a class break, someone stole his money. Derek left school early, but his bike had a flat tire, so he took a taxi. When he got to his apartment, he remembered he didn't have any money to pay the driver. Fortunately, his neighbor paid the fare for him.

*Part II.* Make true sentences. Write one negative and one affirmative statement.

1. Derek woke up feeling good.  *He didn't wake up feeling good. He woke up sick / with a sore throat, etc.*

2. He broke a glass on the floor. _____

   _____

3. He ate a delicious breakfast. _____

   _____

4. He took the bus to school. _____

   _____

5. He left school late. _____

   _____

6. He took the bus home. _____

   _____

7. He paid the driver. _____

   _____

▶ **Practice 25. Review of yes/no questions: past and present.** (Charts 3-9 and 8-8)
Make yes/no questions.

1. _____Do they play_____ tennis?  Yes, they do.  They play tennis.

2. _____Did they play_____ tennis?  Yes, they did.  They played tennis.

3. _____ tennis?  Yes, she does.  She plays tennis.

4. _____ tennis?  Yes, she did.  She played tennis.

5. _____ to work?  Yes, he does.  He walks to work.

6. _____ to work?  Yes, he did.  He walked to work.

7. _____ at home?  Yes, she does.  She works at home.

8. _____ at home?  Yes, she did.  She worked at home.

9. _____ your new job?  Yes, I do.  I like my new job.

10. _____ your old job?  Yes, I did.  I liked my old job.

▶ **Practice 26. Yes/no questions.** (Charts 8-3 and 8-8)
Complete each sentence with **did**, **was**, or **were**.

Tell me about your trip.

1. _____Did_____ you have a good time?

2. _____ it fun?

3. _____ you see a lot of interesting sights?

4. _____ you meet many people?

5. _____ the people friendly?

6. _____ you learn a lot?

7. _____ the trip long enough?

8. _____ you want to come home?

9. _____ you ready to come home?

▶ **Practice 27. Review: questions and negatives.** (Charts 8-7 and 8-8)
Make questions and negative sentences from the given sentences.

|  | **Question** | **Negative** |
|---|---|---|
| 1. a. They play. | _Do they play?_ | _They don't play._ |
| b. They played. | _Did they play?_ | _They didn't play._ |

**134** CHAPTER 8

|  |  | | **Question** | **Negative** |
|---|---|---|---|---|

2. a. They help. _____ _____

   b. They helped. _____ _____

3. a. She listens. _____ _____

   b. She listened. _____ _____

4. a. He works. _____ _____

   b. He worked. _____ _____

5. a. The baby cries. _____ _____

   b. The baby cried. _____ _____

6. a. We are sick. _____ _____

   b. We were sick. _____ _____

▶ **Practice 28. Review: Yes/no questions.** (Charts 8-2, 8-3, 8-7, and 8-8)
Make yes/no questions. Give short answers.

1. A: _____*Were you at home last night?*_____

   B: _____*No, I wasn't.*_____ (I wasn't at home last night.)

   A: _____*Did you go to a lake last weekend?*_____

   B: _____*Yes, I did.*_____ (I went to a lake last weekend.)

2. A: _____

   B: _____ (It isn't cold today.)

3. A: _____

   B: _____ (I come to class every day.)

4. A: _____

   B: _____ (Roberto was absent yesterday.)

5. A: _____

   B: _____ (Roberto stayed home yesterday.)

6. A: _____

   B: _____ (Phillip doesn't change his passwords very often.)

7. A: _____

   B: _____ (Mohammed isn't in class today.)

8. A: _____

   B: _____ (He was here yesterday.)

9. A: _____

   B: _____ (He came to class the day before yesterday.)

10. A: _____

    B: _____ (He usually comes to class every day.)

▶ **Practice 29. Irregular verbs: Group 2.** (Chart 8-9)
Check (✓) the sentences that are true for you. Write the present form for each verb in italics.

**Present Form**

1. _____ I *bought* some snack food yesterday. _____*buy*_____

2. _____ I *read* a newspaper last week. _____

3. _____ I *rode* a horse last year. _____

4. _____ I *ran* up some stairs yesterday. _____

5. _____ I *drank* tea yesterday. _____

6. _____ I *caught* a taxi last week. _____

7. _____ I *drove* a car yesterday. _____

8. _____ I *thought* about English yesterday evening. _____

9. _____ I *brought* this book to school last week. _____

10. _____ My teacher *taught* me new vocabulary last week. _____

▶ **Practice 30. Irregular verbs: Group 2.** (Chart 8-9)
Complete each sentence with the simple past tense form of a verb from the box. The number in parentheses tells you how many verbs you can use.

| | | | | |
|---|---|---|---|---|
| bring | catch | drive | ✓ ride | teach |
| buy | drink | read | run | think |

Jane is a teacher.

1. She didn't drive to work yesterday. She _____*rode*_____ her bike to school. (1)

2. In the morning, she _____ math and science to her students. (1)

3. At lunch time, she went home and got her car. She _____ her car to the mall. (1)

4. She _____ a sweater for her husband at a clothing store. (1)

5. She stopped at a café and _____ some coffee. (2)

6. Then she went home and _____ her students' science projects. (1)

7. Before dinner, she put on her running clothes and shoes. She walked outside and _____ down the street to the store. (1)

8. During her run, she _____ about her favorite foods: potato chips, ice cream, and chocolate. (1)

9. But she _____ home healthy foods: chicken, rice, and vegetables. (1)

10. Her husband _____ a cold last week, and she wants to stay healthy. (1)

► **Practice 31. Irregular verbs: Group 3.** (Chart 8-10)
Check (✓) the sentences that are true for you. Write the present form for each verb in italics.

**Present Form**

1. _____ I *flew* in a small airplane last year.     _____ *fly*

2. _____ I *spoke* a little English two years ago.

3. _____ I *took* the bus to school last week.

4. _____ I *paid* bills last month.

5. _____ I *woke up* early this morning.

6. _____ I *broke* my arm when I was a child.

7. _____ I *sent* an email to a friend last week.

8. _____ I *sang* a song this morning.

9. _____ I *left* my home today.

10. _____ I *met* a famous person at a party.

11. _____ A cell phone *rang* in my English class last week.

12. _____ I *heard* a funny story yesterday.

► **Practice 32. Irregular verbs: Group 3.** (Chart 8-10)
Complete each sentence with the simple past tense form of a verb from the box. There is only one correct verb for each sentence.

| | | | | | |
|---|---|---|---|---|---|
| break | hear | meet | ring | sing | take |
| ✓ fly | leave | pay | send | speak | wake |

1. It was 7:00 A.M. Jerry was asleep. A bird _____*flew*_____ into his open bedroom window.

2. Jerry _____ a noise.

3. The noise _____ him up. He saw the bird.

4. The bird looked hurt. Jerry _____ the bird to the veterinarian.*

5. A nurse _____ Jerry in the parking lot and helped him with the bird.

6. Jerry _____ the bird at the vet's office and went to work.

7. An hour later, Jerry's office phone _____. It was the vet.

8. The vet _____ to Jerry. He said, "The bird _____ its wing, but it's okay."

9. Jerry took the bird home. After a week, its wing got better. Jerry put the bird outside. The bird _____ a few songs and flew away. Jerry watched his little friend, feeling both happy and sad.

10. The vet _____ Jerry a bill for a small amount.

11. Jerry happily _____ the bill.

► **Practice 33. Irregular verbs: Group 4.** (Chart 8-11)
Check (✓) the sentences that are true for you. Write the present form for each verb in *italics*.

**Present Form**

1. _____ I *wore* a hat yesterday.          _____*wear*_____

2. _____ I *said* "Good morning" to my teacher yesterday.          _____

3. _____ I *found* money on the street last week.          _____

---
*veterinarian (vet) = an animal doctor.

4. _____ I *lost* something expensive in the past. _____

5. _____ Someone *stole* something expensive from me once. _____

6. _____ I *hung* up my clothes before I went to bed last night. _____

7. _____ I *told* a funny joke last week. _____

8. _____ My classes *began* on time last week. _____

9. _____ I *sold* something on the Internet. _____

10. _____ The last time I paid bills, I *tore* up a check. _____

▶ **Practice 34. Irregular verbs: Group 4.** (Chart 8-11)
Complete each sentence with the simple past tense form of a verb from the box. There is only one correct verb for each sentence. Note the use of **tell** and **say**: **tell** + person but **say** + **to** + person.

| ✓begin | hang | say | steal | tell |
|--------|------|-----|-------|------|
| find | lose | sell | tear | wear |

1. Martha's school day _____ *began* _____ with bad news.

2. Her husband said, "The dog _____ your students' work into small pieces. Now he's looking at your leather jacket."

3. Martha _____ her leather jacket to school every day. It was her favorite jacket.

4. She picked up her jacket and the homework, and _____ the dog, "No."

5. She went to school. She took off her jacket and _____ it up on a hanger in the closet.

6. At the end of the day, there was no jacket. A student _____ to her, "Maybe a thief _____ it."

7. Someone else said to her, "Maybe you left it somewhere else and don't remember. Maybe you _____ it."

8. Martha wondered, "Did someone steal it? Maybe someone _____ it for money."

9. An hour later, another student _____ Martha's jacket in the closet. It was on a hanger under another teacher's jacket!

► **Practice 35. Review: -ed spelling.**
Write the correct spelling of the **-ed** form.

|  | **-ed form** |  | **-ed form** |
|---|---|---|---|
| 1. wait | _____waited_____ | 9. point | _____ |
| 2. spell | _____spelled_____ | 10. pat | _____ |
| 3. kiss | _____kissed_____ | 11. shout | _____ |
| 4. plan | _____ | 12. reply | _____ |
| 5. join | _____ | 13. play | _____ |
| 6. hope | _____ | 14. touch | _____ |
| 7. drop | _____ | 15. end | _____ |
| 8. add | _____ | 16. dance | _____ |

► **Practice 36. Verb review: simple past tense.** (Chapter 8)
Complete the sentences. Use the verbs in parentheses.

1. Mari and I (*go*) _____went_____ to the pharmacy yesterday. I (*buy*)
_____ some aspirin and (*pick up*) _____ a
prescription.

2. I had to go downtown yesterday. I (*catch*) _____ the bus in front
of my apartment and (*ride*) _____ to Grand Avenue. Then I
(*get off*) _____ the bus and transferred to another one. It (*be*)
_____ a long trip.

3. Sue (*eat*) _____ popcorn and (*drink*) _____ a soft
drink at the movie theater last night. I (*eat, not*) _____ anything.
Movie theater prices are too high.

4. Maria (*ask*) _____ the teacher a question in class yesterday. The
teacher (*think*) _____ about the question for a few minutes and then
said, "I don't know."

5. I (*want*) _____ to go to the basketball game last night, but I (*stay*)
_____ home because I had to study.

6. Last night I (*read*) _____ an interesting article online. It (*be*)
_____ about the superstorm.

7. Rita (*pass, not*) _____ the test yesterday. She (*fail*)
_____ it.

8. Last summer we (*drive*) _____ to Colorado for our vacation. We (*visit*) _____ a national park, where we (*camp*) _____ out in a tent for a week. We (*go*) _____ fishing one morning. I (*catch*) _____ a big fish, but my husband (*catch, not*) _____ anything. We (*enjoy*) _____ cooking and eating the fish for dinner. It (*be*) _____ delicious. I like fresh fish.

▶ **Practice 37. Verb review: past and present.** (Chapters 1–4 and 8)
Complete the sentences with the words in parentheses. Use the simple present, present progressive, or simple past. The sentence may require an affirmative statement, a negative statement, or a question form.

1. Tom (*walk*) _____ *walks* _____ to work almost every day.

2. I can see Tom from my window. He's on the street below. He (*walk*) _____ to work right now.

3. (*Tom, walk*) _____ to work every day?

4. (*you, walk*) _____ to work every day?

5. I usually take the bus to work, but yesterday I (*walk*) _____ to my office.

6. On my way to work yesterday, I (*see*) _____ an accident.

7. Alex (*see, not*) _____ the accident.

8. (*you, see*) _____ the accident yesterday?

9. Tom (*walk, not*) _____ to work last week. The weather was too cold. He (*take*) _____ the bus.

10. I (*walk, not*) _____ to work last week either.

► **Practice 38. Verb review: past and present.** (Chapters 1–4 and 8)
Complete the sentences. Use the words in parentheses. Use any appropriate verb form.

1. I (*finish, not*) _____*didn't finish*_____ my chores last night. I (*go*)
   _____ to bed early.

2. Jasmin (*stand, not*) _____ up right now. She (*sit*)
   _____ down.

3. The weather (*be, not*) _____ cold today, but it (*be*)
   _____ cold yesterday.

4. It (*rain, not*) _____ right now. The rain (*stop*)
   _____ a few minutes ago.

5. Tina and I (*go, not*) _____ shopping yesterday. We (*go*)
   _____ shopping last Monday.

6. I (*go*) _____ to a party last night, but I (*enjoy, not*)
   _____ it. It (*be, not*) _____ a lot of fun.

7. I (*write*) _____ a paragraph for my history class last night, but I
   (*spend, not*) _____ much time on it.

8. My husband (*come, not*) _____ home for dinner last night.

9. The twins (*go*) _____ to bed a half an hour ago. They (*sleep*)
   _____ now.

10. We (*be*) _____ late for a meeting at our son's school last
    night. The meeting (*start*) _____ at 7:00, but we (*arrive, not*)
    _____ until 7:15.

11. Olga (*ask*) _____ Hamid a question a few minutes ago, but he
    (*answer, not*) _____ her.

12. When Ben and I (*go*) _____ to the mall yesterday,
    I (*buy*) _____ some new shoes. Ben (*buy, not*)
    _____ anything.

13. A: What did you do yesterday?

    B: Well, I (*wake up*) _____ around 9:00 and (*go*)
    _____ shopping. While I was downtown, someone (*steal*)
    _____ my purse. I (*take*) _____
    a taxi home. When I (*get*) _____ out of the taxi, I (*tear*)
    _____ my blouse. I (*borrow*) _____
    some money from my roommate to pay the taxi driver.

A: Did anything good happen to you yesterday?

B: Let me think. Yeah. I (lose) _____ my grammar book, but I (find) _____ it later.

14. A: May I use your laptop?

B: Sure.

A: Thanks. I (want) _____ to look for apartment rentals. I (need) _____ to find a new apartment.

15. A: I (see, not) _____ you yesterday. (be) _____ you sick?

B: No, but my daughter (feel, not) _____ well, so I (be) _____ home with her. She's fine now. She (be) _____ at school.

A: That's good to hear.

16. A: Wait! Where (go, you) _____?

B: My dentist's office just (call) _____. Someone (pick) _____ up my wallet in the parking lot. I (need) _____ to go get it.

A: Wow! You're lucky.

B: I (know) _____.

# Appendix 1
## *Irregular Verbs*

| SIMPLE FORM | SIMPLE PAST | SIMPLE FORM | SIMPLE PAST |
|---|---|---|---|
| be | was, were | keep | kept |
| become | became | know | knew |
| begin | began | leave | left |
| bend | bent | lend | lent |
| bite | bit | lose | lost |
| blow | blew | make | made |
| break | broke | meet | met |
| bring | brought | pay | paid |
| build | built | put | put |
| buy | bought | read | read |
| catch | caught | ride | rode |
| choose | chose | ring | rang |
| come | came | run | ran |
| cost | cost | say | said |
| cut | cut | see | saw |
| do | did | sell | sold |
| draw | drew | send | sent |
| drink | drank | shake | shook |
| drive | drove | shut | shut |
| eat | ate | sing | sang |
| fall | fell | sit | sat |
| feed | fed | sleep | slept |
| feel | felt | speak | spoke |
| fight | fought | spend | spent |
| find | found | stand | stood |
| fly | flew | steal | stole |
| forget | forgot | swim | swam |
| get | got | take | took |
| give | gave | teach | taught |
| go | went | tear | tore |
| grow | grew | tell | told |
| hang | hung | think | thought |
| have | had | throw | threw |
| hear | heard | understand | understood |
| hide | hid | wake up | woke up |
| hit | hit | wear | wore |
| hold | held | win | won |
| hurt | hurt | write | wrote |

# Appendix 2
## English Handwriting

| English Handwriting | |
|---|---|
| PRINTING | CURSIVE |
| Aa Jj Ss<br>Bb Kk Tt<br>Cc Ll Uu<br>Dd Mm Vv<br>Ee Nn Ww<br>Ff Oo Xx<br>Gg Pp Yy<br>Hh Qq Zz<br>Ii Rr | Aa Jj Ss<br>Bb Kk Tt<br>Cc Ll Uu<br>Dd Mm Vv<br>Ee Nn Ww<br>Ff Oo Xx<br>Gg Pp Yy<br>Hh Qq Zz<br>Ii Rr |

Vowels = *a, e, i, o, u*
Consonants = *b, c, d, f, g, h, j, k, l, m, n, p, q, r, s, t, v, w, x, y, z*★

---

★The letter *z* is pronounced "zee" in American English and "zed" in British English.

# Appendix 3
## Numbers

CARDINAL NUMBERS

| | |
|---|---|
| 1 | one |
| 2 | two |
| 3 | three |
| 4 | four |
| 5 | five |
| 6 | six |
| 7 | seven |
| 8 | eight |
| 9 | nine |
| 10 | ten |
| 11 | eleven |
| 12 | twelve |
| 13 | thirteen |
| 14 | fourteen |
| 15 | fifteen |
| 16 | sixteen |
| 17 | seventeen |
| 18 | eighteen |
| 19 | nineteen |
| 20 | twenty |
| 21 | twenty-one |
| 22 | twenty-two |
| 23 | twenty-three |
| 24 | twenty-four |
| 25 | twenty-five |
| 26 | twenty-six |
| 27 | twenty-seven |
| 28 | twenty-eight |
| 29 | twenty-nine |
| 30 | thirty |
| 40 | forty |
| 50 | fifty |
| 60 | sixty |
| 70 | seventy |
| 80 | eighty |
| 90 | ninety |
| 100 | one hundred |
| 200 | two hundred |
| 1,000 | one thousand |
| 10,000 | ten thousand |
| 100,000 | one hundred thousand |
| 1,000,000 | one million |

ORDINAL NUMBERS

| | |
|---|---|
| 1st | first |
| 2nd | second |
| 3rd | third |
| 4th | fourth |
| 5th | fifth |
| 6th | sixth |
| 7th | seventh |
| 8th | eighth |
| 9th | ninth |
| 10th | tenth |
| 11th | eleventh |
| 12th | twelfth |
| 13th | thirteenth |
| 14th | fourteenth |
| 15th | fifteenth |
| 16th | sixteenth |
| 17th | seventeenth |
| 18th | eighteenth |
| 19th | nineteenth |
| 20th | twentieth |
| 21st | twenty-first |
| 22nd | twenty-second |
| 23rd | twenty-third |
| 24th | twenty-fourth |
| 25th | twenty-fifth |
| 26th | twenty-sixth |
| 27th | twenty-seventh |
| 28th | twenty-eighth |
| 29th | twenty-ninth |
| 30th | thirtieth |
| 40th | fortieth |
| 50th | fiftieth |
| 60th | sixtieth |
| 70th | seventieth |
| 80th | eightieth |
| 90th | ninetieth |
| 100th | one hundredth |
| 200th | two hundredth |
| 1,000th | one thousandth |
| 10,000th | ten thousandth |
| 100,000th | one hundred thousandth |
| 1,000,000th | one millionth |

# Appendix 4
## Days/Months/Seasons

| DAYS | ABBREVIATION | MONTHS | ABBREVIATION | SEASONS* |
|------|-------------|--------|-------------|----------|
| Monday | Mon. | January | Jan. | winter |
| Tuesday | Tues. | February | Feb. | spring |
| Wednesday | Wed. | March | Mar. | summer |
| Thursday | Thurs. | April | Apr. | fall or autumn |
| Friday | Fri. | May | May | |
| Saturday | Sat. | June | Jun. | |
| Sunday | Sun. | July | Jul. | |
| | | August | Aug. | |
| | | September | Sept. | |
| | | October | Oct. | |
| | | November | Nov. | |
| | | December | Dec. | |

*Seasons of the year are only capitalized when they begin a sentence.

**WRITING DATES:**

### Month/Day/Year

10/31/41  =  October 31, 1941
4/15/98   =  April 15, 1998
7/4/1906  =  July 4, 1906
7/4/07    =  July 4, 2007

**SAYING DATES:**

| Usual Written Form | Usual Spoken Form |
|--------------------|-------------------|
| January 1 | January first / the first of January |
| March 2 | March second / the second of March |
| May 3 | May third / the third of May |
| June 4 | June fourth / the fourth of June |
| August 5 | August fifth / the fifth of August |
| October 10 | October tenth / the tenth of October |
| November 27 | November twenty-seventh / the twenty-seventh of November |

# Appendix 5

## Two-Syllable Verbs: Spelling of -ED and -ING

| VERB | SPEAKING STRESS | | |
|---|---|---|---|
| (a) visit | **VIS** · it | | |
| (b) admit | ad · **MIT** | | |

Some verbs have two syllables. In (a): *visit* has two syllables: *vis + it*. In the word *visit*, the stress is on the first syllable. In (b): the stress is on the second syllable in the word *admit*.

| VERB | STRESS | -ED FORM | -ING FORM |
|---|---|---|---|
| (c) visit | **VIS** · it | visited | visiting |
| (d) open | **O** · pen | opened | opening |
| (e) admit | ad · **MIT** | admitted | admitting |
| (f) occur | oc · **CUR** | occurred | occurring |

For two-syllable verbs that end in a vowel and a consonant:
• The consonant is not doubled if the stress is on the first syllable, as in (c) and (d).

• The consonant is doubled if the stress is on the second syllable, as in (e) and (f).

### COMMON VERBS

| Stress on first syllable: | | | | Stress on second syllable: | | | |
|---|---|---|---|---|---|---|---|
| VERB | STRESS | -ED FORM | -ING FORM | VERB | STRESS | -ED FORM | -ING FORM |
| answer | **AN** · swer | answered | answering | prefer | pre · **FER** | preferred | preferring |
| happen | **HAP** · pen | happened | happening | permit | per · **MIT** | permitted | permitting |
| listen | **LIS** · ten | listened | listening | refer | re · **FER** | referred | referring |
| offer | **OF** · fer | offered | offering | begin | be · **GIN** | (no -ed form) | beginning |
| enter | **EN** · ter | entered | entering | | | | |

# Index

# Answer Key

## CHAPTER 1

### PRACTICE 1, p. 1.
2. She is late.
3. It is difficult.
4. He is sick.
5. She is also sick.
6. He is ready.
7. It is cold.
8. She is single.

### PRACTICE 2, p. 1.
1. is
2. am
3. are
4. is
5. is
6. is
7. is
8. are
9. is
10. is

### PRACTICE 3, p. 2.
3. B
4. B
5. A
6. A, B

### PRACTICE 4, p. 2.
2. are
3. is
4. is
5. is
6. are
7. are
8. are
9. are
10. are

### PRACTICE 5, p. 2.
3. She
4. He
5. She
6. They
7. We
8. We
9. She
10. You
11. They
12. They
13. She
14. He
15. We

### PRACTICE 6, p. 3.
2. a
3. a
4. an
5. a
6. an
7. an
8. a
9. a
10. an

### PRACTICE 7, p. 3.
2. a   yes
3. a   no
4. an  yes
5. a   yes
6. a   no
7. a   yes
8. a   yes

### PRACTICE 8, p. 4.
2. dogs
3. languages
4. machines
5. countries
6. seasons
7. dictionaries

### PRACTICE 9, p. 4.
3. Russian and Spanish are languages.
4. China is a country.
5. South America is a continent.
6. Dogs are animals.
7. Bangkok is a city.
8. Thailand is a country.

### PRACTICE 10, p. 4.
3. Ø . . . Ø
4. Ø . . . Ø
5. s . . . s
6. Ø . . . Ø
7. Ø . . . s
8. Ø . . . Ø . . . s
9. Ø . . . Ø . . . s

### PRACTICE 11, p. 5.
2. is
3. are
4. are
5. is
6. are
7. is
8. are
9. are
10. is
11. are

### PRACTICE 12, p. 5.
2. am a student
3. are a student
4. are students
5. are students
6. is a student
7. are students
8. are students
9. are students
10. are students

## PRACTICE 13, p. 6.
2. Africa is a continent.
3. Asia and Africa are continents.
4. Paris is a city.
5. Cairo is a city.
6. Paris and Cairo are cities.
7. Malaysia is a country.
8. Japan and Malaysia are countries.

## PRACTICE 14, p. 6.
3. is a language
4. are languages
5. are countries
6. is a country
7. is an insect (also correct: an animal)
8. are insects (also correct: animals)
9. is a machine
10. are machines
11. is a city
12. are cities

## PRACTICE 15, p. 7.
2. you're
3. he's
4. we're
5. it's
6. they're
7. she's

## PRACTICE 16, p. 7.
2. are not
3. is not
4. is not
5. is not
6. is not
7. are not
8. are not
9. are not
10. are not
11. is not
12. are not

## PRACTICE 17, p. 7.
2. is not     isn't OR she's not
3. am not     I'm not
4. is not     isn't OR he's not
5. is not     isn't
6. is not     isn't OR it's not
7. are not     aren't OR we're not
8. are not     aren't OR you're not
9. are not     aren't OR they're not

## PRACTICE 18, p. 8.
2. is
3. is
4. isn't
5. are
6. aren't
7. is
8. are
9. aren't
10. isn't

## PRACTICE 19, p. 8.
2. aren't . . . 're machines
3. is . . . isn't
4. aren't . . . 're seasons
5. isn't . . . 's a language
6. 'm not . . . 'm a student
7. 're . . . 're

## PRACTICE 20, p. 8.
2. isn't
3. are
4. aren't
5. isn't . . . is
6. is/isn't . . . is/isn't
7. is/isn't . . . is/isn't
8. aren't . . . are
9. is . . . isn't
10. aren't . . . are

## PRACTICE 21, p. 9.
2. A circle is round.  It isn't square.
3. A piano is heavy.  It isn't light.
4. Potato chips aren't sweet.  They are salty.
5. The Sahara Desert is large.  It isn't small.
6. The Nile River isn't short.  It is long.
7. This exercise is/isn't easy.  It is/isn't difficult.
8. My grammar book is/isn't new.  It is/isn't old.
9. Electric cars are/aren't expensive.  They are/aren't cheap.

## PRACTICE 22, p. 10.
2. at; <u>at the train station</u>
3. from; <u>from Kuwait</u>
4. on; <u>on my desk</u>
5. in; <u>in her purse</u>
6. on; <u>on First Street</u>
7. next to; <u>next to the bank</u>
8. under; <u>under my desk</u>
9. between; <u>between my cheeks</u>
10. on; <u>on the third floor</u>
11. above; <u>above Mr. Kwan's apartment</u>

## PRACTICE 23, p. 10.

## PRACTICE 24, p. 10.

| Nouns | Adjectives | Prepositions |
|---|---|---|
| city | easy | at |
| country | empty | between |
| parents | happy | next to |
| sister | hungry | on |
| teacher | single | outside |

## PRACTICE 25, p. 11.
*Sample answers:*
2. a girl.
   at home.
   nice.
3. big.
   in Asia.
   a country.
4. on the desk.
   clear.
   a textbook.

## PRACTICE 26, p. 11.
2. Canada is in North America.
3. France is next to Germany.
4. The downstairs of a building isn't above the upstairs.
5. Ice isn't hot.
6. Apples and oranges aren't vegetables.
7. Airplanes are fast.
8. Vegetables are healthy.
9. An alligator is dangerous.
10. Alligators aren't friendly.

## PRACTICE 27, p. 12.
| | |
|---|---|
| 2. are | 5. are |
| 3. is | 6. are |
| 4. is | 7. are |

## PRACTICE 28, p. 12.
| | |
|---|---|
| 2. is | 6. is |
| 3. is | 7. am |
| 4. am | 8. is |
| 5. is | 9. am |

# CHAPTER 2

## PRACTICE 1, p. 13.
| | |
|---|---|
| 2. c | 7. c |
| 3. b | 8. c |
| 4. b | 9. b |
| 5. a | 10. c |
| 6. c | |

## PRACTICE 2, p. 13.
2. Is he a student?
3. Are they students?
4. Is she from New Zealand?
5. Are you ready?
6. Are we ready?
7. Is it ready?
8. Am I ready?

## PRACTICE 3, p. 14.
2. Are bananas healthy?
3. Is Taka a nurse?
4. Are the kids at school?
5. Are you/we ready for the test?
6. Is Liz at school?
7. Are you tired?

## PRACTICE 4, p. 14.
| | |
|---|---|
| 2. they are | 7. she is |
| 3. they are | 8. I am |
| 4. he is | 9. we are |
| 5. they are | 10. you are |
| 6. it is | |

## PRACTICE 5, p. 15.
| | |
|---|---|
| 2. Is . . . is | 7. Are . . . are |
| 3. Is . . . is | 8. Are . . . are |
| 4. Is . . . is | 9. Are . . . am |
| 5. Are . . . are | 10. Are . . . are |
| 6. Is . . . is | |

## PRACTICE 6, p. 15.
1. Is Paris a country? No, it isn't.
2. Are October and November months? Yes, they are.
3. Is soccer a season? No, it isn't.
4. Are fall and winter seasons? Yes, they are.

## PRACTICE 7, p. 16.
2. isn't
3. Are Rosa and Dong . . . they are
4. Is Rosa . . . isn't
5. Is Dong . . . he is
6. Is Rosa . . . she is
7. Is Dong . . . isn't
8. Are Rosa and Dong . . . aren't

## PRACTICE 8, p. 16.
1. A: Are you
2. A: Are you
   B: aren't . . . 're
   B: he isn't . . . 's

## PRACTICE 9, p. 17.
2. b
3. a
4. b
5. a
6. b

## PRACTICE 10, p. 17.
2. Is the teacher in the classroom?
3. Where are Pablo and Dina?
4. Are Pablo and Dina at home?
5. Is the map in the car?
6. Where is the store?
7. Are you outside?
8. Where are you?

## PRACTICE 11, p. 18.
| | |
|---|---|
| 2. have | 7. has |
| 3. has | 8. has |
| 4. has | 9. have |
| 5. has | 10. have |
| 6. has | 11. have |

## PRACTICE 12, p. 18.
| | |
|---|---|
| 2. has | 7. has |
| 3. have | 8. have |
| 4. have . . . has | 9. has . . . has |
| 5. has . . . has | 10. has |
| 6. have . . . have | 11. have |

## PRACTICE 13, p. 19.
| 1. *My apartment* | 2. *My neighbor* |
|---|---|
| c. is | a. is |
| d. is | b. has |
| e. has | c. is |
| f. is | d. has |
| g. is | e. has |
| h. has | f. is |
| i. has | g. is |
| | h. is |
| | i. has |

**PRACTICE 14, p. 19.**
2. are . . . have
3. am . . . have
4. are . . . have
5. has . . . is

**PRACTICE 15, p. 20.**
2. has
3. has
4. have
5. has
6. have
7. has
8. is

**PRACTICE 16, p. 20.**
2. Your
3. My
4. Our
5. Your
6. Their
7. Their
8. His
9. Her
10. Their
11. Our
12. Our

**PRACTICE 17, p. 21.**
2. Her
3. His
4. Their
5. Her
6. Their

**PRACTICE 18, p. 21.**
2. have . . . Your
3. have . . . Their
4. have . . . Our
5. has . . . His
6. has . . . Her
7. has . . . His
8. have . . . Their
9. have . . . My
10. have . . . Their

**PRACTICE 19, p. 22.**
2. That
3. That
4. This
5. This
6. That
7. This
8. That

**PRACTICE 20, p. 23.**
2. These
3. Those
4. Those
5. These
6. Those

**PRACTICE 21, p. 23.**
1. These
2. Those
3. This
4. Those
5. That
6. These
7. This

**PRACTICE 22, p. 23.**
2. These . . . Those
3. This . . . That
4. These . . . That
5. This . . . That
6. These . . . Those
7. This . . . Those

**PRACTICE 23, p. 24.**
2. a
3. b
4. a
5. b
6. b

**PRACTICE 24, p. 24.**
2. What is that?
3. What are these?
4. Who are they?
5. What are those?
6. Who is that?

**PRACTICE 25, p. 25.**
2. This is Donna.
3. Yes, it is.
4. Yes, she is.
5. No, it isn't.
6. Yes, he is.
7. It's in Norway.
8. Yes, I am.
9. This is an insect.

**PRACTICE 26, p. 25.**
2. Their
3. her
4. their
5. His

**PRACTICE 27, p. 26.**
2. is
3. has
4. is
5. is
6. is
7. is
8. has
9. is
10. is
11. is
12. am
13. am
14. have
15. are

# CHAPTER 3

**PRACTICE 1, p. 27.**
2. wake
3. wake
4. wakes
5. wake
6. wakes
7. wakes
8. wakes
9. wake
10. wakes
11. wakes
12. wake

**PRACTICE 2, p. 27.**
teaches, leaves, catches, comes, takes, begin, teaches, stays, drives, gets

**PRACTICE 3, p. 28.**
2. get
3. makes
4. cooks
5. leave
6. drive
7. listen to
8. work
9. arrive
10. come
11. take

## PRACTICE 4, p. 28.

2. wake
3. eat
4. eats
5. leaves
6. take
7. cooks
8. falls
9. eat
10. fall
11. see
12. have

## PRACTICE 5, p. 29.

2. I rarely eat breakfast.
3. The students seldom buy their lunch at school.
4. They usually bring lunch from home.
5. My husband and I often go out to a restaurant for dinner.
6. My husband sometimes drinks coffee with dinner.
7. We never have dessert.

## PRACTICE 6, p. 29.

2. Roger seldom/rarely gets up late.
3. Mr. and Mrs. Phillips usually go to the movies on weekends.
4. I often clean my apartment.
5. My roommate never cleans our apartment.
6. The students always do their homework.
7. The teacher sometimes corrects papers on weekends.

## PRACTICE 9, p. 31.

2. I pay my phone bill once a month.
3. I exercise once a day.
4. I visit my cousins twice a year.
5. Dr. Williams checks her email three times a day.
6. The Browns take a long vacation once a year.
7. Cyndi gives dinner parties twice a month.
8. Sam buys vegetables at the farmers' market twice a week.

## PRACTICE 10, p. 32.

2. often . . . Ø
3. Ø . . . sometimes
4. Ø . . . rarely
5. rarely . . . Ø
6. Ø . . . usually
7. usually . . . Ø
8. never . . . Ø
9. never . . . Ø
10. Ø . . . always

## PRACTICE 11, p. 32.

2. The students often help the teacher.
3. The classroom is always clean.
4. The parents usually visit the class.
5. The parents sometimes help the students with their work.
6. The parents are always helpful.
7. The classroom is seldom quiet.

## PRACTICE 12, p. 33.

| -s | -es |
|---|---|
| eats | finishes |
| listens | fixes |
| sleeps | kisses |
| talks | wishes |

## PRACTICE 13, p. 33.

2. teaches
3. mix
4. mixes
5. misses
6. miss
7. brush
8. brushes
9. wash
10. washes
10. cooks
12. reads
13. watches
14. begins
15. come
16. comes

## PRACTICE 14, p. 34.

2. studies
3. study
4. studies
5. study
6. study
7. studies
8. study
9. studies
10. study

## PRACTICE 15, p. 34.

| -ies | -s |
|---|---|
| flies | enjoys |
| studies | pays |
| tries | plays |
| worries | says |

## PRACTICE 16, p. 34.

2. brushes
3. closes
4. fly
5. flies
6. stops
7. fixes
8. call . . . calls
9. studies
10. helps

## PRACTICE 17, p. 35.

1. b. does homework at 10:00.
   c. goes to work at 11:00
2. a. has class at 10:00.
   b. does homework at 11:00
   c. goes to work at 2:00
3. a. do homework at 9:00.
   b. have class at 11:00
   c. go to work at 1:00.

## PRACTICE 18, p. 36.

2. catches
3. gets
4. works
5. fixes
6. come
7. finishes
8. often meets
9. helps
10. usually have
11. goes
12. has
13. is often
14. enjoys

## PRACTICE 19, p. 36.

2. Ø
3. Ø
4. -s
5. -s
6. Ø
7. -s
8. -s
9. Ø
10. Ø
11. -s
12. Ø
13. -s
14. -s
15. -s
16. Ø

## PRACTICE 20, p. 37.
(*Answers may vary.*)

| *need* | *want* |
|---|---|
| electricity | diamond jewelry |
| food | a digital camera |
| money | an expensive house |
| a place to live | a leather coat |
| water | a smartphone |
| | a sports car |

## PRACTICE 21, p. 37.

**Part I.**
*Infinitives:*
wants to have
needs to have
wants to do
needs to take
wants to skip
wants to have

**Part II.**
1. a, b
2. a, b, c
3. d, e

## PRACTICE 22, p. 38.
2. to watch
3. to play
4. to talk to
5. to go . . . to cash
6. to do
7. to wash
8. to go . . . to buy
9. to marry
10. to take
11. to eat
12. to listen to
13. to swim
14. to pay

## PRACTICE 23, p. 39.
1. don't eat
2. don't have . . . don't eat . . . aren't
3. doesn't have . . . doesn't eat . . . isn't
4. doesn't have . . . doesn't eat . . . isn't
5. doesn't have . . . doesn't eat . . . isn't
6. don't have . . . don't eat . . . aren't
7. don't have . . . don't eat . . . aren't

## PRACTICE 24, p. 39.
2. You don't need more time.
3. They don't eat breakfast.
4. Yoshi doesn't like bananas.
5. Susan doesn't do her homework.
6. We don't save our money.
7. The printer doesn't work.
8. The coffee doesn't taste good.
9. Mr. and Mrs. Costa don't drive to work.

## PRACTICE 25, p. 40.
3. doesn't have
4. breaks
5. don't grow
6. doesn't walk
7. cries
8. don't fly
9. don't have
10. helps
11. doesn't fix
12. fixes
13. don't like
14. chase
15. isn't
16. rains
17. doesn't rain
18. don't wash
19. washes

## PRACTICE 26, p. 41.
**Part I.**
2. Mark watches TV.
3. Tom walks to school.
4. Tom, Janet, and Mark study grammar.
5. Janet goes shopping.

**Part II.**
7. Tom and Janet don't watch TV.
8. Mark doesn't skip lunch.
9. Janet doesn't eat dinner at home.
10. Tom and Mark don't eat dinner out.

## PRACTICE 27, p. 41.
2. knows . . . doesn't know
3. want . . . don't want
4. isn't . . . doesn't want
5. doesn't drink . . . drinks
6. am not . . . don't have
7. doesn't belong . . . belongs
8. don't live . . . have
9. is . . . isn't . . . don't need
10. is . . . don't have
11. doesn't eat . . . isn't
12. read . . . don't watch
13. doesn't read . . . watches

## PRACTICE 28, p. 42.
2. Do they study?
3. Does he know?
4. Does the doctor know?
5. Do we know?
6. Do I understand?
7. Do you understand?
8. Does the manager understand?
9. Does your roommate work?
10. Does the car work?
11. Does it work?
12. Do I care?
13. Does she care?

## PRACTICE 29, p. 43.
1. b. Does he play soccer?
   d. Does he lift weights?
2. a. Does he run?
   b. Does he swim/play soccer?
   c. Does he lift weights?
3. a. Do they play soccer?
   b. Do they swim?
   c. Do they run?

## PRACTICE 30, p. 44.
| | |
|---|---|
| 2. a | 6. b |
| 3. b | 7. a |
| 4. b | 8. b |
| 5. a | |

## PRACTICE 31, p. 44.
2. Does he fix . . . he doesn't
3. Do you fly . . . I don't
4. Do you teach . . . we don't
5. Do you clean . . . we don't
6. Do they design . . . they don't
7. Does she write . . . she doesn't
8. Do you work . . . I don't
9. Do they build . . . they don't
10. Does he play . . . he doesn't

## PRACTICE 32, p. 45.

2. Is
3. Does
4. Do
5. Is
6. Do
7. Do
8. Do
9. Do
10. Are

## PRACTICE 33, p. 46.

1. B: am
   A: Are
   B: am
   B: don't
2. A: Do
   B: do . . . is
3. A: Are
   B: am
   A: Do
   A: Do
   B: don't
4. A: Are
   A: Are
   A: are
   B: are
5. A: Is
   B: isn't
   A: is
   A: Is
   B: isn't
   A: is
6. A: are . . . Do
   B: Are
   A: aren't
   B: Are
   B: are

## PRACTICE 34, p. 47.

1. Where
2. Where
3. What
4. What
5. Where
6. What
7. Where
8. What

## PRACTICE 35, p. 47.

2. What does the teacher want?
3. Where does Dr. Varma stay?
4. Where do you catch the bus?
5. What does Lillian need?
6. What do the children want?
7. Where do the construction workers eat lunch?
8. Where are Victoria and Franco?
9. What does Mark bring his wife every week?
10. What do you need?

## PRACTICE 36, p. 48.

2. Where does he work in the summer?
3. What does he look for?
4. Where does he stay?
5. Where does he work in the winter?
6. What does he teach?
7. Where does he live?
8. What does he love?

## PRACTICE 37, p. 49.

3. When
4. What
5. Where
6. When
7. What
8. What
9. When
10. Where

## PRACTICE 38, p. 49.

2. Do you get up early?
3. When does the bus come?
4. Does it come on time?
5. Where do you work?
6. When do you start work?
7. When do you leave work?
8. Do you like your job?
9. Is it interesting?
10. Are you a doctor?

## PRACTICE 39, p. 50.

2. What does he teach?
   He teaches biology and chemistry.
3. Where does he teach chemistry?
   He teaches chemistry in the chemistry lab.
4. When is he in the chemistry lab?
   He's in the chemistry lab at 12:00.
5. Where does he teach biology?
   He teaches biology in the biology lab.
6. Is he in his office every day?
   No, he isn't.
7. Is he in his office at 1:00?
   Yes, he is.
8. Does he teach at 8:00?
   No, he doesn't.
9. When does he teach?
   He teaches at 9:00, 10:00, and 12:00.

## PRACTICE 40, p. 51.

3. studies
4. don't have
5. doesn't clean
6. tastes
7. costs
8. know
9. don't want
10. A: look
    B: am not

## PRACTICE 41, p. 51.

2. Where is she?
3. Are Susie and Johnny at home?
4. Where are they?
5. What time/When is dinner?
6. What does Jane have for dinner?

## PRACTICE 42, p. 52.

2. b
3. a
4. c
5. c
6. c
7. a
8. b
9. b
10. c

# CHAPTER 4

## PRACTICE 2, p. 53.

2. is
3. am
4. is
5. is
6. are
7. are
8. is
9. are
10. are
11. are
12. is
13. is
14. are

## PRACTICE 3, p. 54.

2. winning
3. joining
4. signing
5. flying
6. paying
7. studying
8. getting
9. waiting
10. writing

## PRACTICE 4, p. 54.

2. coming
3. looking
4. taking
5. biting
6. hitting
7. hurting
8. clapping
9. keeping
10. camping

## PRACTICE 5, p. 55.

2. are sitting
3. are talking
4. is doing
5. is reading
6. are kicking
7. is coming
8. are going

## PRACTICE 6, p. 55.

### Part I
3. He is working at his computer.
4. He is talking on the phone.
5. He isn't riding a horse.
6. He isn't buying food for dinner.

### Part II
1. They are talking to patients.
2. They aren't washing cars.
3. They aren't watching movies.
4. They are working with doctors.
5. They are giving medicine to patients.

## PRACTICE 8, p. 57.

2. Are you working?
3. Are they leaving?
4. Is she staying home?
5. Are we going to school?
6. Is the computer working?
7. Is it working?
8. Am I driving?
9. Is your friend coming?
10. Are the students laughing?
11. Is Mr. Kim sleeping?
12. Is Monica dreaming?

## PRACTICE 9, p. 57.

2. A: Is he running
   B: he isn't . . . is driving
3. A: Are they studying
   B: they aren't . . . are swimming
4. A: Is she teaching
   B: she isn't . . . is shopping
5. A: Is she fishing
   B: she isn't . . . is sleeping
6. A: Are they working
   B: they aren't . . . are playing
7. A: Are you washing dishes
   B: I'm not . . . am reading a book.

## PRACTICE 10, p. 58.

### Part I
2. are working

3. is working
4. are working
5. is working

### Part II
7. are not working
8. is not working
9. are not working
10. is not working

### Part III
12. Is . . . working
13. Are . . . working
14. Are . . . working
15. Is . . . working

## PRACTICE 11, p. 59.

### Part I.
2. work
3. works
4. work
5. works

### Part II.
7. do not work
8. does not work
9. do not work
10. does not work
12. Does . . . work
13. Do . . . work
14. Do . . . work
15. Does . . . work

## PRACTICE 12, p. 60.

3. every day
4. every day
5. now
6. now
7. every day
8. now
9. now
10. every day

## PRACTICE 13, p. 60.
*Checked sentences: 2, 6, 8, 9*

## PRACTICE 14, p. 60.

2. am looking
3. are fishing
4. is sitting
5. are playing
6. are swimming
7. are jumping
9. walk
10. go
11. am working
12. work
13. write
14. am writing

## PRACTICE 15, p. 61.

2. Are
3. Is
4. Are
5. Do
6. Is
7. Does
8. Do
9. Does
10. Do
11. Does
12. Do
13. Are
14. Do

## PRACTICE 16, p. 61.
2. smell
3. is crying . . . wants
4. tastes . . . like
5. are running . . . likes . . . hates

## PRACTICE 17, p. 62.
1. think
2. A: does Jan want
   B: needs . . . wants
3. A: Do you hear
   B: hear . . . don't see
4. A: loves
   B: don't believe . . . loves

## PRACTICE 18, p. 62.
| | |
|---|---|
| 2. a | 6. a |
| 3. a | 7. a |
| 4. b | 8. b |
| 5. b | 9. a |

## PRACTICE 19, p. 63.
2. is playing
3. is also listening
4. (is) looking
5. is wearing
6. is talking
7. is telling
8. isn't listening
9. doesn't hear
10. is listening

## PRACTICE 20, p. 63.
2. hear
3. hear
4. listen to
5. A: look at
   B: look at . . . watch
6. A: Do you see
   B: see

## PRACTICE 22, p. 64.
2. a
3. b
4. b
5. a

## PRACTICE 23, p. 64.
1. B: am thinking about
   A: think that
2. A: think that
   B: don't think that . . . think that
3. A: am thinking about
   B: Are . . . thinking about
   B: think that
   A: think that

## PRACTICE 24, p. 65.
1. rings . . . doesn't answer . . . doesn't want . . . believes
2. flies . . . is flying
3. A: Are you waiting
   B: am
   A: does the bus stop
   A: Is it usually
   B: rarely comes

4. A: does your teacher usually do
   B: think . . . corrects . . . has
   A: is she doing
   B: is talking
5. A: Do you know
   B: believe . . . is
   B: know

## PRACTICE 25, p. 66.
| | |
|---|---|
| 1. is sitting | 22. usually exercises |
| 2. is looking at | 23. is thinking about |
| 3. is working | 24. is |
| 4. is studying | 25. smells |
| 5. listening to | 26. wants |
| 6. hears | 27. to watch |
| 7. isn't listening to | 28. is |
| 8. is thinking about | 29. needs |
| 9. is memorizing | 30. to go |
| 10. likes | 31. is eating |
| 11. thinks | 32. is |
| 12. understands | 33. is sleeping |
| 13. is | 34. is dreaming about |
| 14. doesn't like | 35. is playing |
| 15. is cooking | 36. doesn't see |
| 16. cooks | 37. is looking at |
| 17. is cutting | 38. is singing |
| 18. is rising | 39. isn't listening to |
| 19. is standing | 40. hears |
| 20. is taking off | 41. likes |
| 21. is wearing | 42. to listen to |

# CHAPTER 5

## PRACTICE 1, p. 68.
2. What time is it?
3. What's the date (today)?
4. What year is it?
5. What month is it?
6. What time is it?
7. What's the date (today)?

## PRACTICE 2, p. 68.
2. b
3. b
4. a
5. b

## PRACTICE 3, p. 69.
1. b. at
2. a. at
   b. in
   c. on
3. a. in
   b. at
   c. from . . . to
   d. on
   e. on
4. a. in
   b. on
   c. in
   d. at . . . in
   e. on
   f. in

## PRACTICE 4, p. 70.
2. at
3. from . . . to
4. on
5. in
6. at
7. in
8. on
9. from . . . to

## PRACTICE 5, p. 70.
### Part I.
2. How's the weather / What's the weather like in Sydney?
3. How's the weather / What's the weather like in Seoul?
4. How's the weather / What's the weather like in Sydney?
5. How's the weather / What's the weather like in Moscow?

### Part II.
7. no
8. no
9. no
10. yes
11. no

## PRACTICE 6, p. 71.
1. like
2. How's
3. temperature
4. temperature
5. the weather

## PRACTICE 7, p. 71.
2. a
3. b
4. a
5. a
6. b
7. a

## PRACTICE 8, p. 71.
2. are
3. is
4. is
5. are
6. are
7. is
8. is
9. are

## PRACTICE 9, p. 72.
2. There is one couch.
3. There is one table.
4. There are four books.
5. There is one lamp.
6. There are two pillows.

## PRACTICE 10, p. 72.
2. Is       Yes, there is./No, there isn't.
3. Are      Yes, there are./No, there aren't.
4. Is       Yes, there is./No, there isn't.
5. Are      Yes, there are./No, there aren't.
6. Are      Yes, there are./No, there aren't.
7. Is       Yes, there is./No, there isn't.
8. Are      Yes, there are./No, there aren't.
9. Is       Yes, there is./No, there isn't.

## PRACTICE 11, p. 73.
2. Is there a bus station?
3. Are there fast-food restaurants?
4. Are there movie theaters?
5. Is there a park?
6. Are there places to exercise?
7. Is there a visitor information office?

## PRACTICE 12, p. 73.
2. girls
3. cars
4. words
5. minutes
6. seconds
7. stars
8. snowflakes

## PRACTICE 13, p. 74.
2. How many states are there
3. How many colors are there
4. How many countries are there (3 countries = Canada, U.S., Mexico)
5. How many letters are there
6. How many main languages are there

## PRACTICE 14, p. 74.
2. How many exercises are there in this chapter? There are 25.
3. How many pages are there in your dictionary? There are . . . .
4. How many students are there in your class? There are . . . .
5. How many males are there in your class? There are . . . .
6. How many females are there in your class? There are . . . .
7. How many teachers are there at your school? There are . . . .

## PRACTICE 15, p. 75.
2. in
3. on
4. at
5. on
6. in
7. on
8. at

## PRACTICE 16, p. 75.
1. in . . . in
2. in
3. in . . . in
4. at
5. at
6. at . . . at
7. in
8. in
9. in
10. in

## PRACTICE 17, p. 75.
2. at
3. at
4. in
5. in
6. in
7. at
8. in
9. in
10. in

**PRACTICE 18, p. 76.**
2. in
3. in . . . at
4. at . . . in
5. in
6. at . . . at (*"in" is also possible.*)
7. in

**PRACTICE 19, p. 76.**
2. in front of
3. behind/in back of
4. on/on top of
5. next to/beside/near
6. above
7. under
8. between

**PRACTICE 20, p. 77.**
*Sample answers:*
2. On the floor.
3. On my desk.
4. On my book.
5. On my desk.
6. In my hand.

**PRACTICE 21, p. 77.**
2. would like
3. would like
4. would like
5. would like
6. would like
7. would like
8. would like
9. would like
10. would like
11. would like
12. would like

**PRACTICE 22, p. 78.**
2. like
3. likes
4. wants
5. like
6. want

**PRACTICE 23, p. 78.**
3. *no change*
4. Mark would like to get married this year.
5. He would like a pet this year too.
6. *no change*
7. What would he like first?

**PRACTICE 24, p. 79.**
*Part I.*
1. Mary is sleeping. She's dreaming about John.
2. John is sleeping. He's dreaming about Mary.
3. Mary and John are sleeping and dreaming (about each other).
4. I see an alarm clock, two pillows, John and Mary, and two beds.
5. Yes, she is. She's in her bedroom.
6. No, he isn't in class. He's in his bedroom.
7. He's lying down.

8. Yes, she's dreaming.
9. Yes, they are dreaming about each other.
10. Yes, they are in love.

*Part II.*
11. are . . . in
12. is . . . about . . . is . . . about . . . are . . . about
13. on
14. aren't
15. are . . . aren't
16. in
17. to

**PRACTICE 25, p. 79.**

| | |
|---|---|
| 2. a | 8. c |
| 3. a | 9. b |
| 4. c | 10. b |
| 5. d | 11. d |
| 6. d | 12. d |
| 7. a | 13. b |

# CHAPTER 6

**PRACTICE 1, p. 81.**
*Checked words:* 5, 6, 7, 8, 9

**PRACTICE 2, p. 81.**
store, list, eggs, bananas, rice, tea, cell
(*Note: Mike and Judy are also nouns.*)

**PRACTICE 3, p. 81.**
2. Snow
3. The sun
4. The children . . . their parents
5. Some people
6. Teenagers

**PRACTICE 4, p. 82.**
3. patients . . . patients
4. milk . . . milk
5. drink . . . Ø (*Note: objects are nouns.*)
6. their mothers . . . mothers

**PRACTICE 5, p. 82.**
2. c. soccer
3. b. eggs
   c. eggs
4. a. bones
   b. furniture
5. b. lunch
6. a. English
   d. English
7. no objects of verbs
8. b. Maria

**PRACTICE 6, p. 83.**
*Checked phrases:*
3. children
4. table
7. street
9. work
10. house

## PRACTICE 7, p. 83.
Checked sentences:
2. a. <u>backpack</u>
   c. <u>snack</u>
3. b. <u>library</u>
   d. <u>night</u>
4. a. <u>students</u>
   c. <u>classroom</u>

## PRACTICE 8, p. 84.
*Nouns:* car, chair, food, job, leg, rain, tree
*Adjectives:* bright, easy, fresh, nervous, poor, quiet, wet

## PRACTICE 9, p. 84.
2. old
3. hard
4. ugly
5. old
6. interesting
7. slow
8. short
9. hard/difficult
10. quiet

## PRACTICE 10, p. 85.
    A
2. It is very bright.
    N    A      A  N
3. The rooms are large and have tall ceilings.
    N        A    N
4. Her building is next to a Japanese restaurant.
    N       N
5. I love food from other countries.
    A   N   A      A
6. Mexican food is spicy and delicious.
      A   N      N
7. There is a wonderful cafe in my neighborhood.
    N          N
8. My neighbors like to meet there for coffee.

## PRACTICE 12, p. 85.
2. Australia
3. Canada
4. China
5. Egypt
6. India
7. Indonesia
8. Italy
9. Japan
10. Korea
11. Malaysia
12. Mexico
13. Russia
14. Saudi Arabia

## PRACTICE 14, p. 86.
2. He . . . her
3. She . . . them
4. He . . . them
5. They . . . them
6. They . . . him
7. They . . . her
8. They . . . them
9. They . . . them

## PRACTICE 15, p. 87.
2. her
3. them
4. him
5. me
6. us
7. him/it
8. her/it
9. she
10. he
11. they
12. he
13. you
14. you

## PRACTICE 16, p. 87.
2. it
3. them
4. him
5. them
6. them
7. it
8. her
9. him

## PRACTICE 17, p. 88.
2. a
3. b
4. b
5. a

## PRACTICE 18, p. 88.
2. They . . . them . . . They . . . it
3. A: her
   B: She . . . her
4. B: I . . . me
   A: he

## PRACTICE 19, p. 89.
3. Her . . . her
4. His . . . him
5. Our . . . us
6. Their . . . them
7. Her/Its . . . her/it
8. His/Its . . . him/it
9. Its/it

## PRACTICE 20, p. 90.
2. me
3. him . . . his
4. it
5. you
6. Our . . . our
7. their

## PRACTICE 21, p. 90.
1. His . . . him
2. their . . . They . . . them . . . their
3. She . . . Her . . . her
4. their . . . Their . . . their
5. I . . . our . . . our . . . us

## PRACTICE 22, p. 91.
2. tomatoes
3. zoos
4. pen
5. babies
6. keys
7. city
8. wife
9. dishes
10. thieves

## PRACTICE 23, p. 91.

| -s | -ies | -ves | -es |
|---|---|---|---|
| coins | babies | leaves | bushes |
| girls | cities | lives | glasses |
| shoes | ladies | thieves | potatoes |
| trays | parties | wives | taxes |

## PRACTICE 24, p. 91.

2. keys
3. classes
4. thieves
5. tests
6. Babies
7. boxes
8. radios
9. parties
10. cats
11. matches
12. textbooks
13. dictionaries
14. lives
15. tops
16. leaves
17. sandwiches

## PRACTICE 25, p. 92.

2. mice
3. women
4. fish
5. feet
6. men
7. children
8. sheep

## PRACTICE 26, p. 93.

*Corrections for incorrect sentences:*
3. My father **is** in the library.
4. **He** is a teacher.
5. My mother **is** a professor.
6. **She** is an excellent professor.
8. The university **has** many interesting and useful classes.

## PRACTICE 27, p. 93.

2. b
3. a
4. d
5. d
6. c
7. b
8. c
9. a
10. d

## PRACTICE 28, p. 94.

2. hers
3. ours
4. mine
5. yours
6. theirs
8. my
9. his
10. their
11. your
12. our

## PRACTICE 29, p. 94.

2. one
3. more than one
4. more than one
5. one
6. one
7. more than one

## PRACTICE 30, p. 95.

2. car . . . Bill
3. desk . . . the teacher
4. schedules . . . the students
5. truck . . . my parents
6. offices . . . the professors

## PRACTICE 31, p. 95.

2. Dan's
3. teacher's
4. sister's
5. Smith's
6. pets'
7. neighbors'
8. mother's

## PRACTICE 32, p. 96.

3. Ø
4. 's
5. Ø
6. Ø
7. 's

## PRACTICE 33, p. 96.

2. Jane's
3. Mike's
4. Ruff's
5. Marie's
6. Belle's
7. John's
8. Jane's

## PRACTICE 34, p. 97.

2. possessive
3. is
4. is
5. possessive
6. is
7. is
8. possessive

## PRACTICE 35, p. 97.

2. a
3. a
4. b
5. a
6. b
7. b

## PRACTICE 36, p. 97.

2. Whose glasses are these?
3. Whose toy is this?
4. Whose keys are these?
5. Whose shoes are these?
6. Whose shirt is this?
7. Whose cell phone is this?
8. Whose pens are these?

## PRACTICE 37, p. 98.

2. Whose
3. Who's
4. Who's
5. Whose
6. Whose
7. Whose
8. Who's
9. Who's
10. Whose

## PRACTICE 38, p. 98.

2. Whose children are those?
3. Who is next?
4. Whose shoes are in the middle of the floor?
5. Who is absent today?
6. Whose package is this?

## PRACTICE 39, p. 99.

2. one
3. more than one
4. one
5. more than one
6. more than one
7. one
8. one
9. more than one

## PRACTICE 40, p. 99.

3. girls' bikes
4. girl's bike
5. children's toys
6. students' passwords
7. woman's wage
8. women's wages
9. people's ideas
10. person's ideas
11. men's coats

# PRACTICE 41, p. 100.

*Corrections for incorrect sentences:*
2. Several students' parents . . .
3. . . . my brother's friends (no apostrophe)
6. . . . other people's opinions
7. Women's opinions . . .
8. your husband (no apostrophe)

# PRACTICE 42, p. 100.

2. d
3. b
4. a
5. c

6. c
7. a
8. d

# CHAPTER 7

# PRACTICE 1, p. 101.

2. P
3. S
4. S
5. P

6. S
7. P
8. S

# PRACTICE 2, p. 101.

2. a, one
3. five, a lot of
4. five, a lot of

5. a, one
6. five, a lot of
7. an, one

# PRACTICE 3, p. 101.

2. C
3. NC
4. NC
5. C

6. NC
7. NC
8. C

# PRACTICE 4, p. 102.

2. a lot of, ten, twenty
3. a lot of
4. a lot of
5. a lot of, ten, twenty
6. a, one
7. a lot of, ten, twenty
8. a lot of

# PRACTICE 5, p. 102.

1. Ø . . . -s . . . -s
2. Ø . . . Ø . . . -s . . . -s
3. Ø . . . Ø . . . Ø
4. Ø . . . Ø . . . -s . . . -s

# PRACTICE 6, p. 102.

2. a, one
3. a lot of
4. a, one
5. an, one
6. a lot of

7. a lot of
8. a, one
9. a lot of
10. a lot of

# PRACTICE 7, p. 102.

2. homework
3. music
4. vocabulary
5. information
6. advice

7. furniture
8. fruit
9. money
10. jewelry

# PRACTICE 8, p. 103.

2. horses
3. cities
4. countries
5. monkeys
6. help
7. traffic
8. children
9. furniture

10. feet
11. fruit
12. potatoes
13. weather
14. work
15. advice
16. men
17. tools

# PRACTICE 9, p. 104.

2. an
3. an
4. a
5. an
6. an

7. an
8. a
9. a
10. an

# PRACTICE 10, p. 104.

3. Ø
4. an
5. a
6. an

7. an
8. Ø
9. Ø
10. Ø

# PRACTICE 11, p. 105.

2. a
3. Ø
4. an
5. Ø
6. A
7. a
8. an . . . an

9. Ø
10. a
11. Ø
12. an
13. an
14. an . . . a

# PRACTICE 12, p. 106.

| *a* | *an* | *some* |
|---|---|---|
| dog | earache | advice |
| flower | elevator | eggs |
| letter | umbrella | furniture |
| suggestion | | gardens |
| | | mail |
| | | packages |
| | | umbrellas |

# PRACTICE 13, p. 106.

3. a          singular
4. some     plural
5. an        singular
6. some     plural
7. some     plural
8. some     plural
9. a          singular
10. some    plural

# PRACTICE 14, p. 107.

2. some
3. Some
4. a
5. an
6. Some

7. a
8. some
9. some
10. an

# PRACTICE 15, p. 107.

2. b
3. a, b
4. a, c

5. b
6. b

**PRACTICE 16, p. 108.**
2. a tube of toothpaste
3. a bar of soap
4. a bunch of bananas
5. a carton of milk
6. a jar of pickles
7. a box of candy
8. a bottle of olive oil
9. a can of corn

**PRACTICE 17, p. 108.**
2. paper
3. lettuce
4. bread, cheese, lettuce, paper
5. bread
6. bananas, lettuce
7. cereal, ice cream, rice
8. water
9. mayonnaise

**PRACTICE 18, p. 109.**
1. b. some
   c. some
   d. a
   e. an
   f. a
   g. some
   h. some
2. b. a
   c. some
   d. a
   e. a
   f. some
   g. some
   h. some

**PRACTICE 19, p. 110.**
2. many
3. much
4. much
5. much
6. much
7. much
8. much
9. many
10. many

**PRACTICE 20, p. 110.**
2. a few
3. a few
4. a little
5. a little
6. a few
7. a few
8. a few
9. a little
10. a few

**PRACTICE 21, p. 110.**
3. a few . . . s
4. a few . . . s
5. much . . . Ø . . . a little . . . Ø
6. many . . . s
7. a few . . . s . . . many . . . s

**PRACTICE 22, p. 111.**
2. How much cheese do we need?
3. How many eggs do we need?
4. How much flour do we need?
5. How much fruit do we need?
6. How much olive oil do we need?

**PRACTICE 23, p. 111.**
1. the
2. The
3. a . . . The . . . the
4. a . . . The . . . the
5. a . . . a . . . a . . . The . . . the
6. a . . . The
7. a . . . The
8. a . . . a

**PRACTICE 24, p. 112.**
2. specific
3. general
4. general
5. specific
6. specific
7. general
8. specific

**PRACTICE 25, p. 112.**
2. The
3. Ø
4. a
5. an
6. Ø
7. an
8. Ø
9. Ø . . . Ø
10. Ø . . . Ø . . . a
11. the
12. Ø . . . a

**PRACTICE 26, p. 113.**
2. b
3. b
4. a
5. b
6. a
7. a

**PRACTICE 27, p. 113.**
2. any
3. some
4. any
5. some, any
6. any
7. some
8. some
9. some, any
10. Some

**PRACTICE 29, p. 114.**
2. any
3. any
4. a
5. any
6. a
7. a
8. any
9. any
10. an
11. any

**PRACTICE 30, p. 115.**
4. any
5. any
6. any
7. a
8. any
9. any
10. any
11. a
12. any
13. a
14. any
15. any
16. a

**PRACTICE 31, p. 115.**
*Draw a line through:*
1. b, d, e
2. a, c, f
3. a, c

**PRACTICE 32, p. 116.**
2. Is there **much traffic** at 5:00 P.M.?
3. Are **you hungry**? Do you want some food?
4. My children come home every day with a lot of **homework**.
5. **Digital** cameras take wonderful pictures.
6. My eggs and coffee don't taste very good. **The** eggs are very salty, and **the** coffee is weak.
7. What do you like better for a snack: **oranges/an orange or orange** juice?

8. I wear dresses for work **and jeans** at home.
9. I'm going to **the** bank. I need money.
10. We need to get **some** furniture. Do you know **a** good furniture store?

# CHAPTER 8

## PRACTICE 1, p. 117.

| | |
|---|---|
| 2. were | 7. were |
| 3. was | 8. were |
| 4. were | 9. was |
| 5. was | 10. were |
| 6. was | |

## PRACTICE 2, p. 117.

| | |
|---|---|
| 2. were | 7. was |
| 3. was | 8. were |
| 4. was | 9. was |
| 5. was | 10. were |
| 6. was | |

## PRACTICE 3, p. 118.

| | |
|---|---|
| 2. weren't | 7. wasn't |
| 3. weren't | 8. weren't |
| 4. weren't | 9. wasn't |
| 5. wasn't | 10. weren't |
| 6. wasn't | 11. weren't |

## PRACTICE 4, p. 118.

| | |
|---|---|
| 2. wasn't | 6. weren't |
| 3. weren't | 7. wasn't |
| 4. weren't | 8. wasn't |
| 5. wasn't | 9. weren't |

## PRACTICE 5, p. 119.
*Some possible answers:*
2. wasn't at school.  He was on vacation.
3. wasn't at work.  She was out of town.
4. weren't at school.  They were out of town.

## PRACTICE 7, p. 119.

| | |
|---|---|
| 2. Was | 7. Was |
| 3. Was | 8. Was |
| 4. Were | 9. Were |
| 5. Were | 10. Were |
| 6. Was | |

## PRACTICE 8, p. 120.
2. A: Was Ellen at the library?
   B: No, she wasn't.
   A: Where was she?
   B: She was at the mall.
3. A: Were you at a party?
   B: No, I wasn't.
   A: Where were you?
   B: I was at home.
4. A: Was Thomas at the airport?
   B: No, he wasn't.
   A: Where was he?
   B: He was at the train station.
5. A: Were your kids at school?
   B: No, they weren't.
   A: Where were they?
   B: They were at the zoo.

6. A: Were Liz and you at the park?
   B: No, we weren't.
   A: Where were you?
   B: We were at the library.

## PRACTICE 9, p. 121.

| | |
|---|---|
| 2. Were | 6. Was |
| 3. Were | 7. Were |
| 4. Was | 8. Were |
| 5. Was | |

## PRACTICE 10, p. 121.

| | |
|---|---|
| 2. studied | 7. talked |
| 3. walked | 8. helped |
| 4. worked | 9. helped |
| 5. smiled | 10. listened |
| 6. smiled | 11. listened |

## PRACTICE 11, p. 122.
2. exercised at a gym.
3. cooked breakfast.
4. talked to friends on the phone.
5. watched TV.

## PRACTICE 12, p. 122.

| *Group A.* | *Group B.* |
|---|---|
| 2. walked | 16. arrived |
| 3. washed | 17. played |
| 4. erased | 18. signed |
| 5. kissed | 19. shaved |
| 6. laughed | 20. smiled |
| 7. stopped | 21. enjoyed |
| 8. finished | 22. closed |
| 9. touched | 23. rained |
| 10. worked | 24. sneezed |
| 11. coughed | 25. remembered |
| 12. cooked | 26. killed |
| 13. asked | |
| 14. helped | |

*Group C.*
28. needed
29. counted
30. invited
31. visited
32. folded
33. waited
34. added

## PRACTICE 13, p. 125.

| | |
|---|---|
| 1. liked | 12. waited |
| 2. closed | 13. pointed |
| 3. shaved | 14. touched |
| 4. loved | 15. melted |
| 5. hated | 16. married |
| 6. exercised | 17. tried |
| 7. planned | 18. hurried |
| 8. dropped | 19. replied |
| 9. clapped | 20. dried |
| 10. joined | 21. stayed |
| 11. shouted | 22. delayed |

## PRACTICE 14, p. 126.

2. rained
3. helped
4. planned
5. dreamed
6. erased
7. closed
8. yawned
9. studied
10. worried
11. dropped

## PRACTICE 15, p. 127.

2. learned
3. tasted
4. waited
5. stopped
6. carried
7. rubbed
8. stayed . . . cried
9. failed
10. smiled
11. clapped

## PRACTICE 16, p. 128.

2. yesterday
3. last
4. last
5. last
6. last
7. yesterday
8. ago
9. ago
10. ago
11. yesterday
12. last

## PRACTICE 17, p. 128.

2. Bonnie walked to the park yesterday/one day ago.
3. Tom was at home on vacation last week/one week ago.
4. Sam graduated from high school four years ago.
5. Jan worked 12 hours two days ago.
6. Thomas stayed with his parents two months ago.
7. We watched a DVD yesterday/last night/one day ago/ yesterday evening.

## PRACTICE 18, p. 129.

2. ate
3. ate
4. ate
5. ate
6. ate
7. ate
8. did
9. did
10. did
11. did
12. slept
13. slept
14. slept
15. slept

## PRACTICE 19, p. 129.

*Present forms:*

2. come
3. go
4. have
5. put
6. sleep
7. see
8. do
9. eat
10. write
11. sit
12. stand

## PRACTICE 20, p. 130.

2. went
3. sat/slept/stood
4. saw
5. got
6. ate/had
7. saw
8. came/got/went
9. wrote
10. put, had

## PRACTICE 22, p. 131.

2. didn't come
3. didn't come
4. didn't come
5. didn't come
6. didn't come
7. didn't play
8. didn't play
9. didn't answer
10. didn't see
11. didn't sleep
12. didn't do
13. wasn't
14. weren't

## PRACTICE 24, p. 133.

*Sample answers:*

2. He didn't break a glass on the floor. He broke a plate.
3. He didn't eat a delicious breakfast. He had breakfast at school.
4. He didn't take the bus to school. He got/took his bike.
5. He didn't leave school late. He left school early.
6. He didn't take the bus home. He took a taxi.
7. He didn't pay the driver. His neighbor paid the driver/paid the fare.

## PRACTICE 25, p. 134.

3. Does she play tennis?
4. Did she play tennis?
5. Does he walk to work?
6. Did he walk to work?
7. Does she work at home?
8. Did she work at home?
9. Do you like your new job?
10. Did you like your old job?

## PRACTICE 26, p. 134.

2. Was
3. Did
4. Did
5. Were
6. Did
7. Was
8. Did
9. Were

## PRACTICE 27, p. 134.

2. a. Do they help?     They don't help.
   b. Did they help?    They didn't help.
3. a. Does she listen?  She doesn't listen.
   b. Did she listen?   She didn't listen.
4. a. Does he work?     He doesn't work.
   b. Did he work?      He didn't work.
5. a. Does the baby cry?  The baby doesn't cry.
   b. Did the baby cry?   The baby didn't cry.
6. a. Are we sick?      We aren't sick.
   b. Were we sick?     We weren't sick.

## PRACTICE 28, p. 135.

2. A: Is it cold today?
   B: No, it isn't.
3. A: Do you come to class every day?
   B: Yes, I do.
4. A: Was Roberto absent yesterday?
   B: Yes, he was.
5. A: Did Roberto stay home yesterday?
   B: Yes, he did.
6. A: Does Phillip change his passwords very often?
   B: No, he doesn't.
7. A: Is Mohammed in class today?
   B: No, he isn't.
8. A: Was he here yesterday?
   B: Yes, he was.
9. A: Did he come to class the day before yesterday?
   B: Yes, he did.
10. A: Does he usually come to class every day?
    B: Yes, he does.

## PRACTICE 29, p. 136.

*Present forms:*
2. read
3. ride
4. run
5. drink
6. catch
7. drive
8. think
9. bring
10. teach

## PRACTICE 30, p. 136.

2. taught
3. drove
4. bought
5. drank/bought
6. read
7. ran
8. thought
9. brought
10. caught

## PRACTICE 31, p. 137.

*Present forms:*
2. speak
3. take
4. pay
5. wake up
6. break
7. send
8. sing
9. leave
10. meet
11. ring
12. hear

## PRACTICE 32, p. 138.

2. heard
3. woke
4. took
5. met
6. left
7. rang
8. spoke . . . broke
9. sang
10. sent
11. paid

## PRACTICE 33, p. 138.

*Present forms:*
2. say
3. find
4. lose
5. steal
6. hang
7. tell
8. begin
9. sell
10. tear

## PRACTICE 34, p. 139.

2. tore
3. wore
4. told
5. hung
6. said . . . stole
7. lost
8. sold
9. found

## PRACTICE 35, p. 140.

4. planned
5. joined
6. hoped
7. dropped
8. added
9. pointed
10. patted
11. shouted
12. replied
13. played
14. touched
15. ended
16. danced

## PRACTICE 36, p. 140.

1. bought . . . picked up
2. caught . . . rode . . . got off . . . was
3. ate . . . drank . . . didn't eat
4. asked . . . thought
5. wanted . . . stayed
6. read . . . was
7. didn't pass . . . failed
8. drove . . . visited . . . camped . . . went . . . caught . . . didn't catch . . . enjoyed . . . was

## PRACTICE 37, p. 141.

2. is walking
3. Does Tom walk
4. Do you walk
5. walked
6. saw
7. didn't see
8. Did you see
9. didn't walk . . . took
10. didn't walk

## PRACTICE 38, p. 142.

1. went
2. isn't standing . . . is sitting
3. isn't . . . was
4. isn't raining . . . stopped
5. didn't go . . . went
6. went . . . didn't enjoy . . . wasn't
7. wrote . . . didn't spend
8. didn't come
9. went . . . are sleeping
10. were . . . started . . . didn't arrive
11. asked . . . didn't answer
12. went . . . bought . . . didn't buy
13. B: woke up . . . went . . . stole . . . took . . . got . . . tore . . . borrowed
    B: lost . . . found
14. want . . . need
15. A: didn't see . . . Were
    B: didn't feel . . . was . . . is
16. A: are you going
    B: called . . . picked . . . need
    B: know

# NOTES

# NOTES

# NOTES

# NOTES

# NOTES

# NOTES

# NOTES

# NOTES

# NOTES

# NOTES